To Ian
All the best
Richard [illegible]

Are We Here Yet?

An investigation into notions of pilgrimage

31° Press

First Published in Great Britain 2011 by 31° Press

Edited by Adam Fine

ISBN 978-0-9567835-0-9

Published with the support of the University of Cumbria,
Arts Council England and the C&C Products Art Fund.

Design and Layout by Michael Coombs

Cover Image: Michael Coombs

Contents

Contributors

David Imrie

David Imrie is currently a freelance researcher/writer based in Glasgow. He was previously Senior Lecturer and Course leader for the MA Community Arts Programme at the University of Cumbria. His research interests include contemporary art and criticality, socially engaged art practice, aesthetic theory and philosophy, urban regeneration and the arts and critical cultural policy. He is hoping to develop a project on Public Spheres in the Contemporary Metropolis.

Michael Coombs

Michael Coombs is an interdisciplinary fine artist working in the fields of landscape and science-based art. His work focuses on how we engage with and embrace the romanticism of landscape and the concepts handed down from physics and cosmology. Michael's work acknowledges his own fascination with these subjects while exploring the role of constructed realities and the fantastic in 21st century culture through combinations of audio, video, photography, text, objects and installations. He is Technician/Demonstrator in Photography at the University of Cumbria.

Rich Webster

Rich Webster took an Art Foundation Course at Jacob Kramer College in Leeds in 1980 and then took 20 gap years spending the '80s as a selfish yuppie and the '90s repenting in exile in France. On his return to the U.K. he continued to make ground as an artist by taking a B.A (Hons) in Fine Art at Cumbria College of Art and Design and then a Masters in Contemporary Fine Art at Cumbria Institute of the Arts.

He considers himself primarily as a painter but has ventured into installation, sculpture, text and photography, which is an important part of his painting process.

He continues to work from his studio in Devon.

On The Road To Somewhere

David Imrie

Two separate but related projects, two different journeys, both framed as 'pilgrimages.' We are presented with reflective words and images, phrases and photographs, souvenirs and fragmentary glimpses of travel. We see snatches of the lyrical and the banal, objects, commodities, emblems and logos, places and landscapes—empty and crowded, movement and rest, crossing points and stopping points, the beautiful, the ugly and the superfluous, traces of chance encounters—all given shape and structure by a particular, self-chosen modality of travel, of journeying through a particular landscape: in one case, 'petrochemical' wanderings around a cinematically informed United States, the other, on foot, along the well-trodden pilgrims' way to Santiago de Compostella in Spain, with detours to our modern temple of consumption, the supermarket. Here we have a pair of modern day, slightly sceptical, self-aware, secular pilgrims in search of what? Michael Coombs and Rich Webster write eloquently of the personal and broader cultural and philosophical motivations behind these projects. They give us visual archives and personal testimony, evocations of wanderings along hallowed and haunted paths and roads, freighted with cultural associations. They start from specifics, but there are wider resonances to be found here—the images and the framing of these peregrinations stimulate further reflection.

Why pilgrimage? In her book *Wanderlust*, Rebecca Solnit sees pilgrims' paths as manifesting a geography of spiritual power. They act as a liminal space where movement through a defined territory brings the spiritual and material worlds into direct proximity. There is a destination—usually some kind of important sacred site—but the "here and nows" of the journey are equally significant. Thinking and doing, belief and action, interior and exterior, body and soul, the physical and the metaphysical come together. An inner journey is given symbolic form, but that inner journey draws on meanings and signs from the outside—the inside and the outside are interdependent. Symbols and signs are given depth. The pilgrimage with its various trials and tests, changing environments, rhythms and climates can be physically challenging, but this material stripping away is supposed to induce a heightened awareness, a directed intensification of our habitual experience and bodily senses. This may be about acknowledging some transcendent force or power, but also about a personally significant psychologically important space of transformation and revelation. In any case, we might be dealing with mindscapes rather than merely detached places or landscapes—backdrops to the normal, everyday routines. In the contemporary world, of course, these are not just the concerns of pilgrims. Our travellers here are following in the footsteps of (and might have been influenced by) a disparate band of wanderers—flaneurs, fuguers, psychogeographers, nomads, land artists, Beat poets and photographers, site-specific interventions, filmmakers, phenomenologists, landscape and urban architects, and planners, shamans and mystics, New

Agers, self-help gurus, assorted spiritual advisors. All in their different and contradictory ways, seeking some provisional re-enchantment and reframing of place and space, a more intense and multi-faceted experience of what surrounds us, what we tend to take for granted—alternative cartographies and paths of desire.

A focus on pilgrimage has always been a key part of the experience of multifarious religions and belief systems—pre-determined itineraries which offer a framework for direct expression of individual and communal faith but also an opportunity for intensified working through of personal struggles and concerns. Jonathan Sumption, one of the historians of medieval pilgrimage, quotes a writer at the end of the 15th century, castigating the (seemingly) excessive devotion of the populace to pilgrimages, reflecting that their principal motives were:

> "curiosity to see new places and experience new things, impatience of servant with his master, of children with their parents, or wives with their husbands." (Sumption, 1975, p.13)[i]

A complex mixture of motivations has always gone into the pursuit of pilgrimage. In the perhaps stifling, pessimistic, death-haunted medieval society that Sumption describes, where forces outside of anyone's control loomed large in everyday existence, supplication and pious acts were seen as necessary acts. Asceticism and self-denial, voluntary exile, expiation of sin through undergoing physical hardships, seeking a more personal, literal understanding of faith, moral reformation and the chance to start afresh, acts of penance and the pursuit of the miraculous all fed into the cult of pilgrimage. This involved a developing tension between private austerity, popular enthusiasm and abstract ritual, to paraphrase Sumption. It also fostered a nascent commodification overlaid on top of the pilgrim routes, themselves sometimes overlaid on top of earlier trading routes. This commodification brought with it various forms of publicity: postcards, pamphlets, guidebooks and travellers' tales, inns and hostels, fairs and carnivals, tokens and badges, special uniforms, offerings and reliquaries, rhymes and jingles—a whole popular material culture accompanying the spiritual journeying, the mystical and the worldly, totally intermingled.

Pilgrimage can then be seen as a frame, which has always brought together the personal, the material and some wider search for transcendent, possibly spiritual meaning, but the spiritual and the 'secular' can be closely intertwined. There may be an element of cultural tourism and consumerism nowadays, though, that is not entirely new. Every chosen route, traditional or invented, brings along with it a set of cultural accretions, palimpsests of historical layers. In turn, these layers become imprints, which are animated by human touches and residues—the personal narratives that add intrigue and emotional density, the differential rhythms, and micro-episodes that bring to life abstract spaces and structures. We can see these two projects, whatever their specificities, as potentially complex 'representational spaces', to draw upon a concept formulated by Henri Lefebvre in *The Production of Space* (1974) as part of a linked triad of key terms. Representational spaces are distinct from spatial practice (our routine, everyday relationship to social space) and representations of space (the dominant, codified forms of knowledge and sign systems). They embody "complex symbolisms, sometimes coded, sometimes not, linked to the clandestine or underground side of everyday life as also to art." (Lefebrve, 1991, p.33)[ii] Moreover, this is space "as directly lived through its associational images and symbols [...] Thus it is the dominated—and hence passively experienced—space which the imagination seeks to change and appropriate. It overlays physical space, making symbolic use of its objects [...]." (Lefebrve, 1991, p.39)[iii] This signifies something "alive. It embraces the *loci* of passion, of action and of lived situations, and thus immediately implies time ... it may be directional, situational or relational, because it is essentially qualitative, fluid and dynamic." (Lefebrve, 1991, p.42)[iv] These particular complex representational spaces draw on these characteristics. They want to us to feel things differently. They can help us focus on things, which sometimes pass us by in the repetitive daily routines of our highly technologically mediated existence. Yet they have to use these technological means to get across their passions, to provide the appropriate sensory equipment that fits the topographies of these journeys through particular places. The photographic images, sometimes as the result of chance as well as the intention of the photographer-artist, draw our attention to patterns and forms, to captured moments.

This is the aesthetic dimension—a dimension of dissensus to follow some of the formulations of philosopher, Jacques Rancière, in his reflections on art and images. (Rancière, 2010)[v] These projects are not just documentary records of the journey undertaken or a form of personal testimony. They are that and more. They weave a new sensory fabric out of the existing, taken for granted, sensible world "re-distributions, re-compositions, and re-configurations of elements" (Rancière, 2009, p.212)[vi], of habitual forms of experience. They add another interlinked chain of micro-events on top of the causal narrative of the pilgrimage with its beginnings, projected ends and the various consequences that come from this. There is a figural displacement that parallels the rearrangements of normal perception that might be part of the pilgrimage, not just a supplement, but a series of new metaphorical associations that are offered to us to make us think about a range of issues, which the artists identify in their essays, but which might best be discerned where words run out—in pictorial silence. We can then read these sites in our own way and construct our own pathways through these recollected wanderings.

The possibility of re-configuring the commonplace might only be provisional or temporary. Pilgrimages come to an end, of sorts. We have to return home, but hopefully changed and challenged by the experience. These two projects challenge us to reconsider what might motivate some of our own journeys and how we choose to capture these in word and image, and attach significance to our surroundings. It is always worth going along for the ride.

Notes to the Text

[i.] Sumption, J. (1975) *Pilgrimage: An Image of Medieval Religion*. Faber and Faber, London. p.13 and passim

[ii.] Lefebrve, H. (1991) *The Production of Space*, translated Donald Nicholson -Smith. Blackwell, Oxford. p.33

[iii.] Lefebrve op cit. p.39

[iv.] Lefebrve op cit. p.42

[v.] See Rancière, J. (2009) *Dissensus: On Politics and Aesthetics*. Edited and translated by Steven Corcoran. Continuum, London.

[vi.] Rancière, J (2009) op cit. p.212 see als Rancière. *The Emancipated Spectator.* Verso, London 2009 and Passim

Michael Coombs

The Faintest Idea

Michael Coombs

Dr. Emmitt Brown has a lot to answer for. I mean if it wasn't for him I doubt I would be here, scrawling notes onto the pages of a very dog-eared notebook in a motel room in Green River, Utah—the predawn light creeping in from behind the torn mesh that partially covers the void left by the open windows, and the rumbling of the trucks pulling into the gas station over the road only just audible over the whirring of the ageing and fairly ineffective air conditioning unit hanging from the wall provide the backdrop, the liminal space that is at the heart of this trip. With a slightly fuzzy head, the result of the previous day's long drive followed by a few too many of the state's specialty beers,[i] and very little sleep, I head out into the burgeoning day with a backpack full of camera kit.

Despite, or maybe because of, the technological advances in the decade or so that has passed since digital photography became the default choice, it was very clear that this was a trip to be documented on film. In this case, a whole stack of 120 roll film that had been sitting on my bookshelves for many years waiting to be either thrown away or, as was to be the case, to provide the warm yellow cast that Kodak film many years past its 'process by' date gives to a road trip across the USA.

So what of 'Doc' Brown? *Back to the Future*, for some of us of the right age to see it in the cinema or in the following years on VHS, it was our first experience of the idea of an historical America, or at least the first to catch our attention. Alternating between a polished vision of California in 1985 and a beguiling image of mid 1950s America complete with its combination of classic cars, 'vintage' fashions and rock 'n' roll in a setting of romanticised conservative cultural values and a steadfast belief in the bright new future it brought this idealised vision of an historical America to life.[ii]

While there are certainly many more influential experiences that have intervened in my life in the last 25 years that have brought me here, from my school art teachers and university lecturers to the perennial influence of Kerouac, Gregory Crewdson, David Lynch's *The Straight Story*, or even The Hold Steady, at the root of it there is still a bit of a Hill Valley tint to my sunglasses.

Destinations and Transcendence

When the idea of this trip was first mooted I wasn't clear as to its purpose, yet I made some decisions about where, when and how it would take place. I deliberately chose not to have an itinerary, just a car, a few dollars for fuel and some food, and the open road. While I felt it had some kind of connotations of pilgrimage it didn't pertain to what most people understand as pilgrimage, secular or otherwise. It didn't have a shrine or holy site as an end; it was, in essence, petrochemical wandering. However, following a brief period of research I embarked on the trip as a pilgrimage which, to my mind at least, had a precedent in the wanderings of the early Celtic Christian *Peregrini* who would also leave their homelands for destinations unknown.[iii] (MacFarlane, 2007)

It is often noted by prospective *peregrini* that the choice of pilgrimage was not a conscious one, but more that it selected them. Indeed this was certainly a notion with which I felt an affinity. While I had no final destination to focus my attention, it was clear to me that for a real road trip, America, or rather the United States of America, to distinguish it from it northern and southern continental counterparts, was the only conceivable location.

So what was the attraction of the USA? In the absence of any first hand experience of the nation beyond some brief acquaintances made while travelling in other parts of the world it was clearly based on the idea of America, its image a culmination of 30 years worth of exposure to its history, culture and mythology through the media of film, television, literature, music, advertising and consumerism. This America is as much an amalgamation of *Back to the Future* and *Twin Peaks* as it is a vague recollection of the principles of the founding fathers, faded monochrome images from the era of the pioneers or the gold rush, or scratchy TV images and sound bites from the Apollo space programme. I was adamant that, in its origins or aims, this trip was some kind of pilgrimage despite the absence of an obvious final destination or traditional object of veneration.

A common theme in discussions as to what differentiates a pilgrimage from any other form of travel often refers back to the idea that a pilgrimage is simultaneously an outward and inward journey, a journey toward some kind of a greater understanding of God. It's an interesting problematic when discussing the idea of secular pilgrimage. With what can we replace this fundamental characteristic that is allied to a secular understanding? One response is that it is self-selecting. It is in effect, that upon which we deem important enough to impart that status of pilgrimage; however, this seems too circular to be the whole answer. It would also be obtuse not to consider the notion that these secular excursions are not pilgrimages at all, rather just another, albeit more directed, more personally significant form of tourism. This suggests that an acceptance of a religious context as being fundamental to the notion of pilgrimage, for many the obvious response to this is that, without religion or faith, we cannot have a true pilgrimage. While this may be true, can we not also have an experience that while not religious performs a comparable function? Perhaps a more analytical view is one that draws us back to the notion of religious pilgrimage as a form of sacrament, *an outwardly visible sign of an inward grace*, an idea that we can transpose onto a secular understanding. To explore this we need to answer the question of what pilgrimages are for; for me at least, there seems to be some kind of answer in an understanding of how the brain works.

The Faintest Idea

We are told that as humans we tend to privilege language in the sphere of meaning, we return to words not only to negotiate the everyday world around us, but that we also tend to resort to words to discuss art and music through a complicated web of semantic linguistic signs and frames. While this may initially seem illogical, it is understandable in the context of the developments in neuroscience and linguistics proposed by Charles J. Fillmore, George Lakoff or Antonio Damasio, who state, and I hope I'm not doing them a disservice here, that a linguistic system of frames and metaphor are hardwired into the way that the brain operates. While sitting in a motel room somewhere to the east of Denver on a humid afternoon in August, I came across a lecture by George Lakoff on one of the myriad of cable TV channels that, in-between tornado warnings for the local area, discussed cognitive science and the role of linguistics in American politics. The 'ordinary conceptual systems' that we use to negotiate the world that he described fitted closely with my thinking about how I understood pilgrimage and indeed America. Lakoff tells us:

> "The brain is structured on frames and conceptual metaphors. Framing is normal. You can't think anything without a frame, and every word is defined relative to such a structure."[iv]
> (Lakoff, 2008)

I have never been completely convinced by the notion that knowledge is inseparable from naming, that in broad terms the function of labelling and categorising is comprehension; however, implicit in Lakoff's statement is the notion that frames can exist independently of language, but all words operate relative to a frame. Wittgenstein shows us the problem of trying to speak about the things that can only be shown.

He leaves us with his famous last proposition in *Tractatus Logico-Philosophicus*: "Whereof one cannot speak, thereof one must be silent". (Wittgenstein, 2002, p.89) This highlights the difficulties we have when explaining how we can have 'ideas' that are used to make decisions and understand the world, yet we have no real way of communicating them except through art. It is however clear that through the process of labelling we link to the frames that are essential to greater or clearer understanding. By this process remote locations or obscure ideas become tangible. To quote Robert MacFarlane: "Naming was and remains a way to place space within a wider matrix of significance; a way, essentially, to make the unknown known." (MacFarlane, 2003, p.191) To me it seems that although we may need to name to give us the ability to discuss things, would it not also be true to say that to experience something either first hand or perhaps even vicariously, through dramatic retelling or emotive imagery, gives us another, a greater, level of understanding? With our first forays away from the planet in the early 1960s and later when Neil Armstrong first stepped onto the moon in 1969 'space' became quantified in our imaginations, just as the Antarctic had with the 'capture' of the south pole by Roald Amundsen and Robert Scott in 1911 and 1912.

Could it be then that a pilgrimage is the process by which we manifest the transcendent or at least give it some frame of reference by which we can describe and understand it? Whilst naming gives us the ability to discuss the tangible, when we come to the *a priori* transcendental (in the Kantian sense),[V] we might think that this realm of self-referential frames would merely lead to circular arguments.

We can say that the notion of a God, defined by his absence (and subsistent faith in his existence) is transcendent. Most of us have had no demonstrable first hand experience of that which we call God. So how do we deal with this absence? How can pilgrimage bring us closer to God? It could be argued that through the act of pilgrimage we provide a 'frame' that goes beyond language but in which the word 'God' finds a greater meaning or significance.

If this system of frames is at the heart of how we all think, we are continually evolving our understanding of a myriad of seemingly unrelated concepts through experiences and gained knowledge. Relative frames and the meaning of words are in a subtle but continual state of flux driven through our actions: personally, socially, nationally and globally. However while these connections are in a sense fluid, intense experiences or repetition render the synaptic links that are triggered as permanent fixtures in our brains:

"Neural connections get stronger the more they are used, and you get certain ideas in your head that won't go away, ever. The brain gets structured."[vi] (Lakoff. 2008)

A pilgrimage is a way of making a series of loose ideas or connections physical, real, there to be drawn upon when we trigger a certain memory.

When I choose to recall the straight black line on the Bonneville salt flats that demarcates the edge of the Southern Californian Timing Associations' 'long course', stretching over the horizon on the rock hard intricate, interlaced web of startlingly bright white salt crystals and the specs of dust and debris around which they have formed, my mind retrieves the disparate elements of that experience from different parts of the brain. The sight of the day-glow red mile markers and the aroma of ethanol, gasoline and hot engine oil merge to reconstruct the experience. The brain recombines these separate elements in to a cohesive memory or recollected experience. This operates so well in fact, we are told that there is currently no real discernible difference between how we think or imagine and how we recollect;[vii] memories can be brought back together and 'experienced' again or drawn upon in part to help build up an idea or scenario you have never encountered.

Part of the memory recollection process seems to include *Concept Neurons*, an old idea that has until recently been dismissed. However, Francis Crick and Christof Koch, as part of their research into the neuronal correlates of consciousness, have examined activity patterns of single neurons in the hippocampus. These neurons are triggered by very specific visual stimuli. The interesting discovery is that these neurons trigger not only at, say an image of a movie star but also at the text of their name. They are triggered by the concept or idea of say Steve McQueen rather than just his image. In some cases neurons were triggered when a subject closely related to the first was shown, for a fan of Mr. McQueen's work, the sight of a Porsche 917 in Gulf livery may also trigger the McQueen neuron yet a 917 in a different livery, one not seen in his 1971 film *Le Mans*, may not. These neurons demonstrate a basis for associative conceptual thinking in memory.

Yet although this extremely complex transfer of ideas and information is achieved through textual language it seems to me that the knowledge obtained through language, and therefore a second generation link to a frame, can not give the kind of full understanding that doing something in physical actuality gives us. We all know from experience that we learn better by doing rather than watching or merely being told. This is the essence of how pilgrimage operates as a means of learning; it is essential to the process of understanding the more obscure, less tangible ideas about who we are or what we do.

It is also interesting to look at the role of mirror neurons here; although there is still some debate as to their role in humans, it is generally accepted that these trigger when you perform an action or when you see someone else perform the same action. These mirror neurons are connected to the emotional regions of the brain, the result is we experience much of what we see happening to others. Firstly this is a biological basis for empathy, but it is also, importantly for this text, that they impart upon us an emotional synergy with those who we see engaged in a familiar experance. It is not a huge leap to suggest that the feelings I experience speeding along the more remote sections of the American road network come in part from my perceived experience of the characters in road movies from *Vanishing Point* to *Two Lane Blacktop* … and maybe somewhere in my pre-motor cortex there is a neuron firing, one that relates to an old man riding across Iowa on a lawn mower to see his sick brother.

So where does this take us? In summary it would seem plausible that a function of pilgrimage is to put an experience into a frame, to strengthen the links between certain concept neurons, or to tap in to, and understand first hand, an experience we have only previously negotiated vicariously through a range of media from word of mouth to film. We can draw upon these events to give us a more succinct description of a loose set of ideas that can make up a relationship with an absent God, or whatever our secular pilgrimages lead us to, modifying a frame that will change the brain and therefore the way we think,— and who we are. Macfarlane was correct: naming something does make it real, but we have to go there to understand it.

Contradiction Games

In the process of trying to understand what this trip was about, I played a game where I would select two 'things'—sometimes words, places, people, films or ideas: one that I felt had an affinity to the idea that I was pursuing in the process of this trip, the *other*—something related to the first thing, but was somehow unconnected. For example, this trip was San Francisco; it was not New York. It was Christopher McCandless; it was not Steve Fossett. It was *Mulholland Drive*; it was not *Blue Velvet*. It was faded shabby motels; it was not hotels. Through this process I documented innumerable, sometimes obscure relationships between contradictory images or ideas, what I would later understand—thanks to Mr. Lakoff—as linguistic frames. I had built up an image of what it was I was trying to explore.

This process felt appropriate when considering the USA as a nation of cultural contractions, of entrenched traditions and an unwavering desire for progress, of community and individualism, freedom, and a kind of Tocquevilleian *tyranny of the majority*, of religion and hedonism, of individuality and of belonging, yet unlike much of the Old World, here it is a sense of belonging with, or an attachment to, a piece of paper: A nation whose *raison d'être* was carved out with pen and ink, rather than from a common ethnicity, or the seemingly infinite historical lineage to a specific geography found in the Old World. However, it can be argued that a nation founded on an ideology is one prone to a degree of vulnerability. To know what America stands for, or rather why it is different, one must know and understand its origins. This is a unity of shared citizenship, but increasingly it appears the nation is looking inward towards it's differences rather than to its unity.

One thing that I was unprepared for upon my arrival in the USA, was the number of flags, the omnipresent star spangled banner on car bumpers, t-shirts, or flying from every conceivable location. If you are anywhere but the remotest locations you would have trouble going 50 yards without coming across one. What were they all for? Was it in case I forgot where I was? Or was it—as the people I spoke to would have me believe—a symbol of a genuine sense of pride at being American and of the things for which it stands? To an outsider whose national flags are only really seen on public buildings, tourists' postcards and for a few weeks every four years during the football world cup,[viii] its ubiquity gives a sense that, much like an overly elaborate apology, it is somehow trying to cover up, or rather to compensate for something.

Like most national flags the stars and stripes are a symbol or frame for the history and the ideology of a country, and in this case its uneasy overemphasis a symbol of the inherent fragility of its foundations in a simultaneously increasingly global society, one that is retreating into non-geographical communities of shared ideology or interest.

However, one of the many benefits of having a national foundation born not of historicism but of design, is that the Constitution seems to have given rise to a kind of sense that if you can create a nation and its ideology, it's certainly possible to create your own personal future and to have a chance of secular immortality though the greatness of some special endeavour. This has long been intrinsic to the American model; yet possibly more interestingly, from my experiences on this trip, it also seems to me that in some way it has lead to the notion that it's also possible to construct your own history, a kind of personal historical revisionism. Idealised histories are part of the American identity, from Elvis, or the Abner Doubleday Cooperstown story, to the products of the film industry.[ix] While scholarly historical revisionism is regarded as part of the ongoing dialogue between the past and present that makes up the subject of history, there is a non-academic, even personal variant that is in itself, by no means unique to the USA but that is somehow embraced here to an even greater extent than elsewhere. This, from my own perspective as an art practitioner and—dare I say it—a romantic, is a fantastically alluring attribute. Where else can one make his or her own past, present and future to suit his or her own ideals and aspirations to such a degree? Something, I'm sure Doc Brown would understand only too well.

Road Trips

Travel can mirror this flexibility of perspective; it can give us a freedom from the mundane, the situations in which we can, not necessarily intentionally, fictionalise events and make our myths. Here all our normal frames of reference are no longer there to rely on. From a social anthropologist's perspective an essential part of travel is the entering of a liminal state where normality is suspended for a given period. This liminal condition is a transitional state in which common rules of social behaviour are relaxed or even deferred. In these situations we lose the greater part of our social identity and status; we become exposed to ambiguity and indeterminacy.

The product of this is not merely to take a break from the structures that we impose on our daily lives: it performs an additional function, even in the case of the American road trip, these experiences of difference and 'other' offer a situation against which we can question and reinterpret the normal.

Although it is clear that not everybody while traveling away from 'home' is cognisant of this condition and likely to make a conscious effort to reevaluate their lives from this detached position; nonetheless it is a function of separation that many people experience regularly, consciously or otherwise, through travel.

It can be argued that contemporary art takes up a permanently liminal position of its own, operating from outside the conventional, where it also gives us the opportunity to examine more closely and to reappraise the situations presented to us. In this way art not only highlights the subject separated from normal frames of reference, but also provides deeper insights into our own hermeneutical interpretational process. This was interesting when considering my view of America.

My America

The America I found was, as expected, an amalgamation of my idealised America, rich in melancholic nostalgia of filmic landscapes, abandoned semi-derelict motels and gas stations on deserted dusty desert highways, of billboards, hamburger joints, and of small town bars where satellite sports TV is always on.

In my head it was predominantly constructed of the romanticised fifties America, portrayed in *Back to the Future*, mixed with remembered passages from *On the Road* first published in the late summer of 1957, through the Marlboro cigarette advertisements seen in my grandparents copies of *National Geographic*, pictures of Craig Breedlove's *Spirit of America* as featured in my picture book of racing cars, given to me for some birthday in my formative years, to the overly colour-saturated film of the build up to the launch of Apollo 11 at Cape Kennedy, as it was then, and to footage of skateboarders in empty Californian backyard pools that inspired me as a teenager.

I was standing in the middle of a sun-baked road, watching the warm late summer sun sink behind the Rockies through the viewfinder of the super8 camera I had borrowed from a friend for the trip, while the celluloid rattled through at 24 frames per second, when it occurred to me that this journey, far from having no real destination, was really a pilgrimage to an idea: the idea of America. It took the form of a series of micro pilgrimages to destinations previously unknown to me, yet they were all too clear when I found them. These places, chanced upon while meandering through this vast nation, were locations or experiences that fitted with my idealised America, those which reinforced or enhanced my myth.

This project explores this ideal of America. A pilgrimage to Dean and Sal, Neil Armstrong, Christopher McCandless, Marty McFly, Kowalski and the road as a *raison d'être*. It is the culmination of 30 years of received Americana and a period spent exploring how the myth fits and modifies the experience of the reality. It is detached from any global credit and banking crisis, while $100 plus barrels of oil only make it feel more poignant. As the idea of America as a land of plenty, providing for and protecting its citizens indefinitely draws to a close, it is at this point that nostalgia for this endangered epoch increases in vigour. Whilst this project explores my America, the pervasive nature of American culture will have left its imprint on most; the language of accompanying images will be readable to all. The path followed by Kerouac has become the foundation for many voyages of self-discovery, and *On the Road* is a manifesto and inspiration for quasi-rebellious road trips throughout the world. In the text, Kerouac's *alter ego*, Sal Paradise, mirrors the 'search' of modern pilgrims, but in an untouchable pre-lapsarian golden age that epitomised this epoch of accelerated achievement, where the notion of frontiersmanship and freedom were reflected in bright chromium.

This trip and the resulting photographs access this enduring vision of the USA built as much on idealised histories as an appetite for a better future, and employs it as a foundation for an analysis of the function of constructed histories and borrowed nostalgia in the 21st century.

So, the outcome of this investigation? It occurs to me that what a pilgrimage is really about is making manifest a sense of identity, a scene of what an individual considers fundamentally important: a physical tribute to somewhere, something or someone who may be long past, but yet we feel there is something in their character or achievement that reflects something of ourselves, or rather something of our idealised self, a statement of what one considers important directed more to ourselves than to others. It is through this process that we manifest the transcendent or at least give some frame of reference to it, through which we can describe and understand it. It gives us a tantalising grasp of some vital *qualia*.

As a result the electrical pulses that join the various regions of my brain, the ones that give us our best guess at what makes up the marvel of consciousness, the ones that make me, *me*, are transformed in some permanent and physical way by these experiences.[x]

Notes to the Text

[i.] If you are ever in Utah and see a bottle of *Squatters Full Suspension* I implore you to try it. At the guidance of my friend Adam 'Tex' Fine, the exploration of regional specialty beers would be a theme we would continue across the myriad of states we passed through.

[ii.] It is interesting to note that we are now approaching a time where the date that *Back to the Future* was released is as distant to us as the 1955 Marty visited was to his native 1985. Yet somehow 1985 does not yet seem to provide the same scope for similar cultural reconstruction or cinematic historical revisionism.

[iii.] According to MacFarlane, R (2008) *The Wild Places*, Granta. p.23-26

[iv.] Lakoff, G, Politics of Language, 2008, US Public Broadcasting Service (PBS) television broadcast, August 2008

[v.] "I call all cognition *transcendental* that is occupied, not so much with objects, but rather with our mode of cognition of object insofar as this is to be possible *a priori*" Kant, I, 1998, *Critique of Pure Reason*, translated by Guyer, P & Wood, A W. Cambridge University Press. p.149 (A12.) and Passim.

[vi.] Lakoff, G, Politics of Language, 2008, US Public Broadcasting Service (PBS) television broadcast, August 2008

[vii.] As discussed in: Schacter, D. Addis D. (2007) 'The cognitive neuroscience of constructive memory: remembering the past and imagining the future', Philosophical Transactions of the Royal Society B. May 2007

[viii.] While I nominally consider the Union Flag to be my national flag, I include the St George's Cross here in reference to England's football team.

[ix.] As has been widely cited in the press including: Birnbaum, M. (2010) 'Texas board approves social studies standards that perceived liberal bias.' *The Washington Post*, 22nd May 2010. Historical revisionism has been shown in a slightly less benign form. Recently conservative elements of the Texas Board of Education approved changes to its history curriculum and textbooks to fit with Conservative moral and political motivations. It was proposed that Texas state schools would omit Thomas Jefferson's philosophical influence from 'world history' lessons as well as the principle of the separation of church and state. Instead classes should teach that the founding fathers intended America to be a Christian nation. Changes will also emphasise the role of key conservative people and groups including Ronald Regan and the Moral Majority and the National Rifle Association.

[x.] As discussed in Massimini, M. Ferrarelli, F. Huber, R. Esser, S.K. Singh, H. and Tononi, G. (2005) 'Breakdown of Cortical Effective Connectivity During Sleep.' *Science*, VOL 309, ISSUE 5744, pp. 2228-2232. The team examined the brain's response to small, targeted, electrical pulses during waking and sleep. They found that under waking conditions the pulses triggered in one region of the brain quickly spread around various other regions of the brain, yet while unconscious these pulses only initiated local responses.

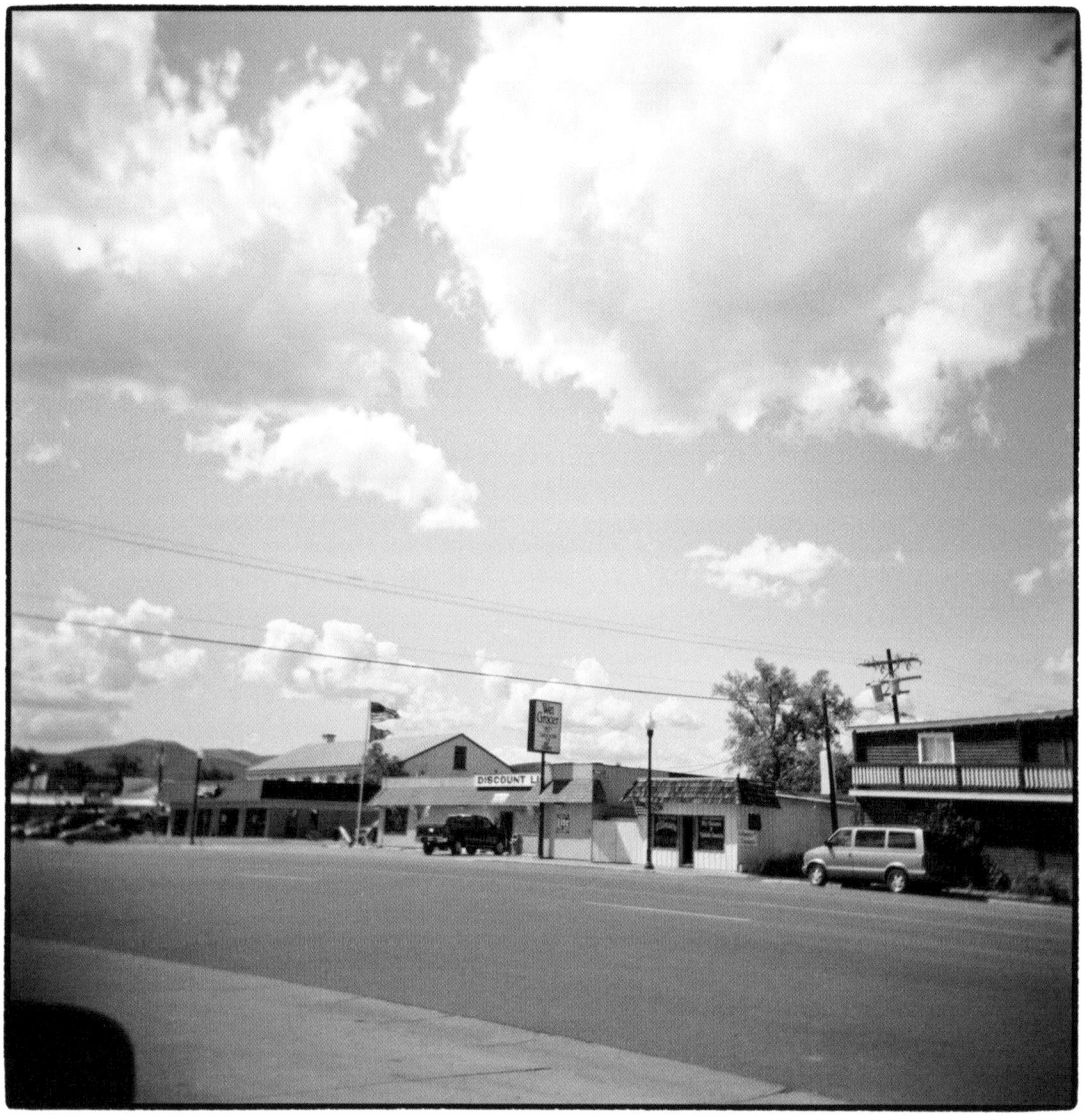
DISCOUNT L

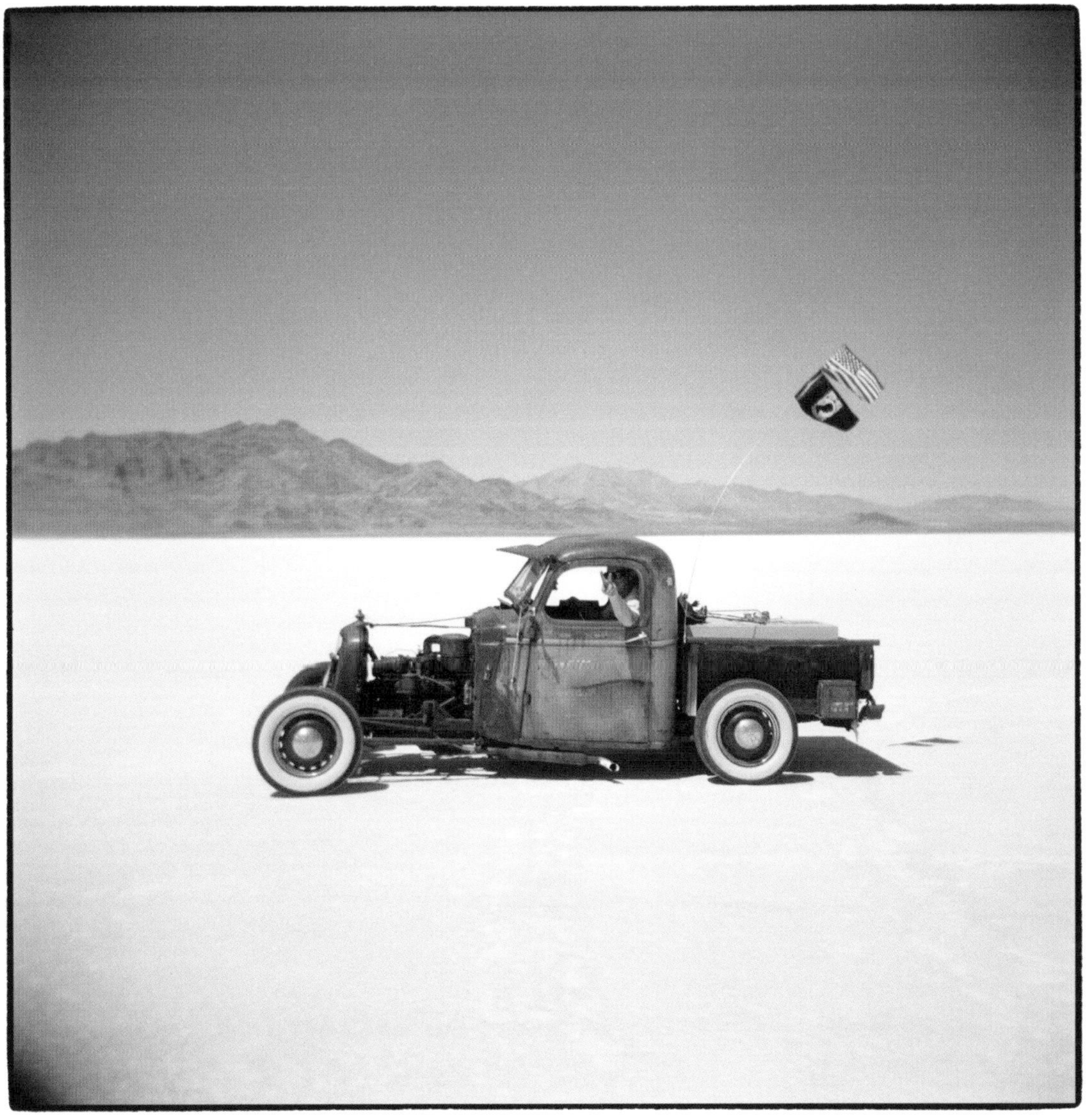

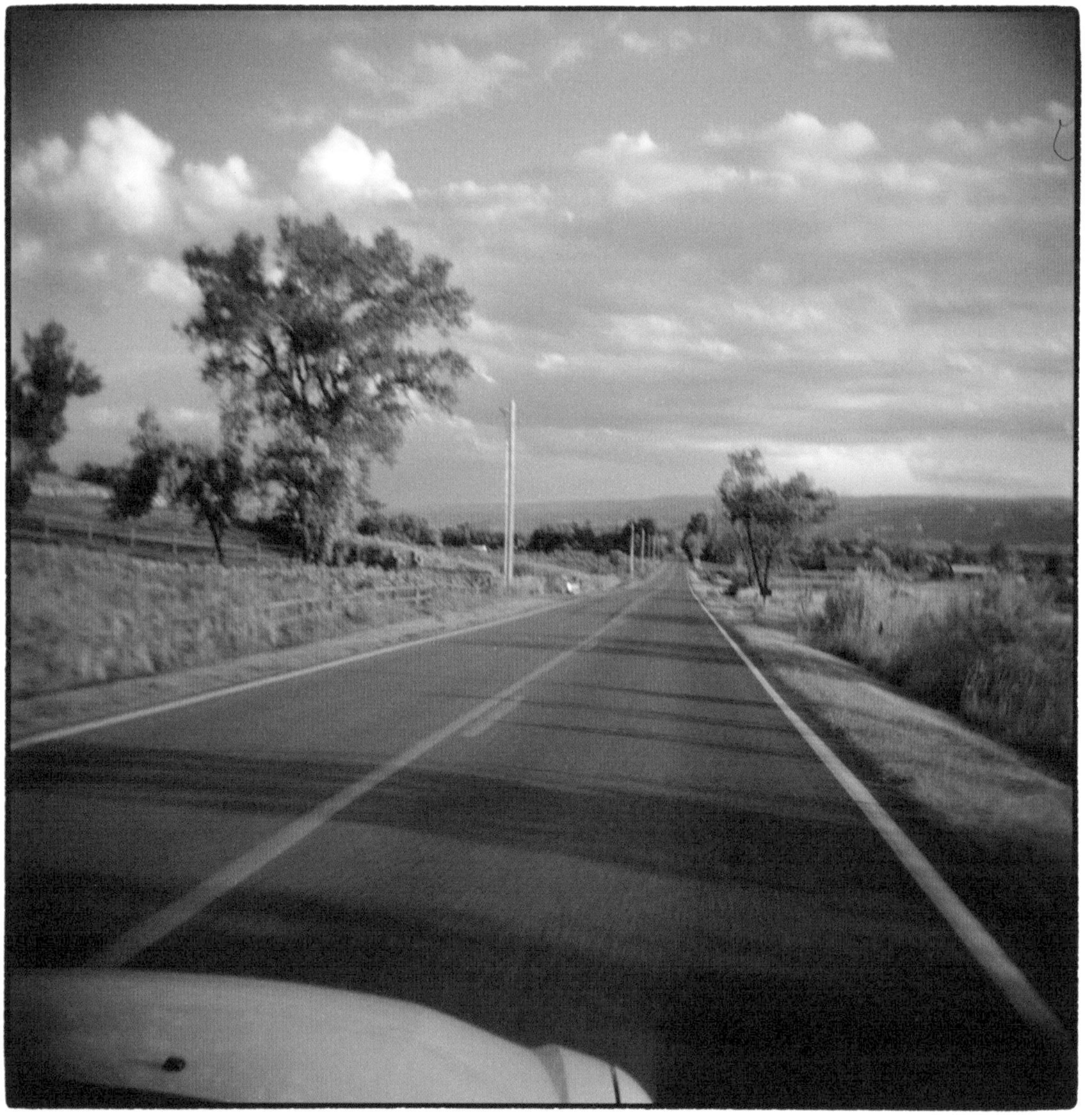

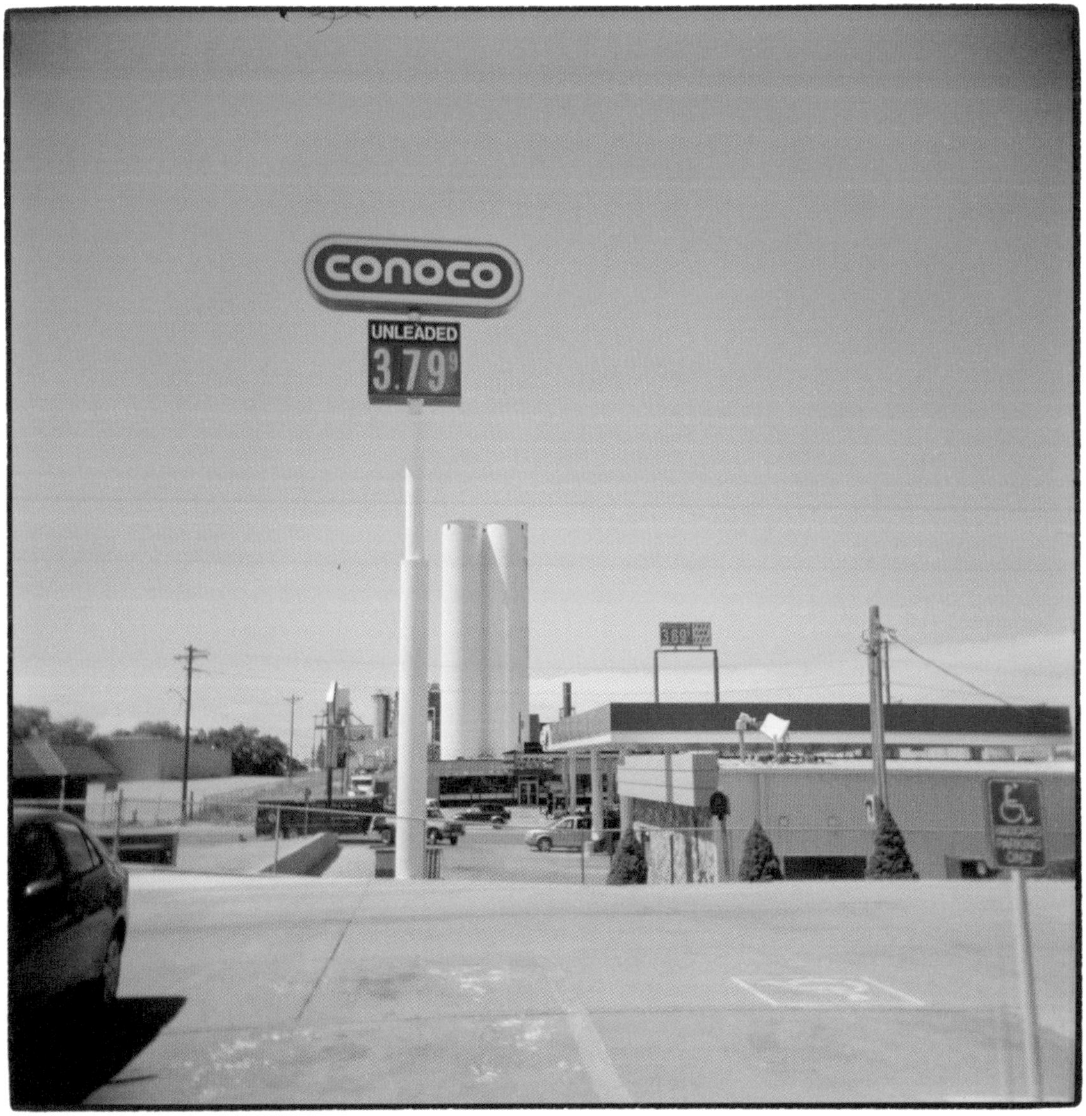
CONOCO
UNLEADED
3.79 9

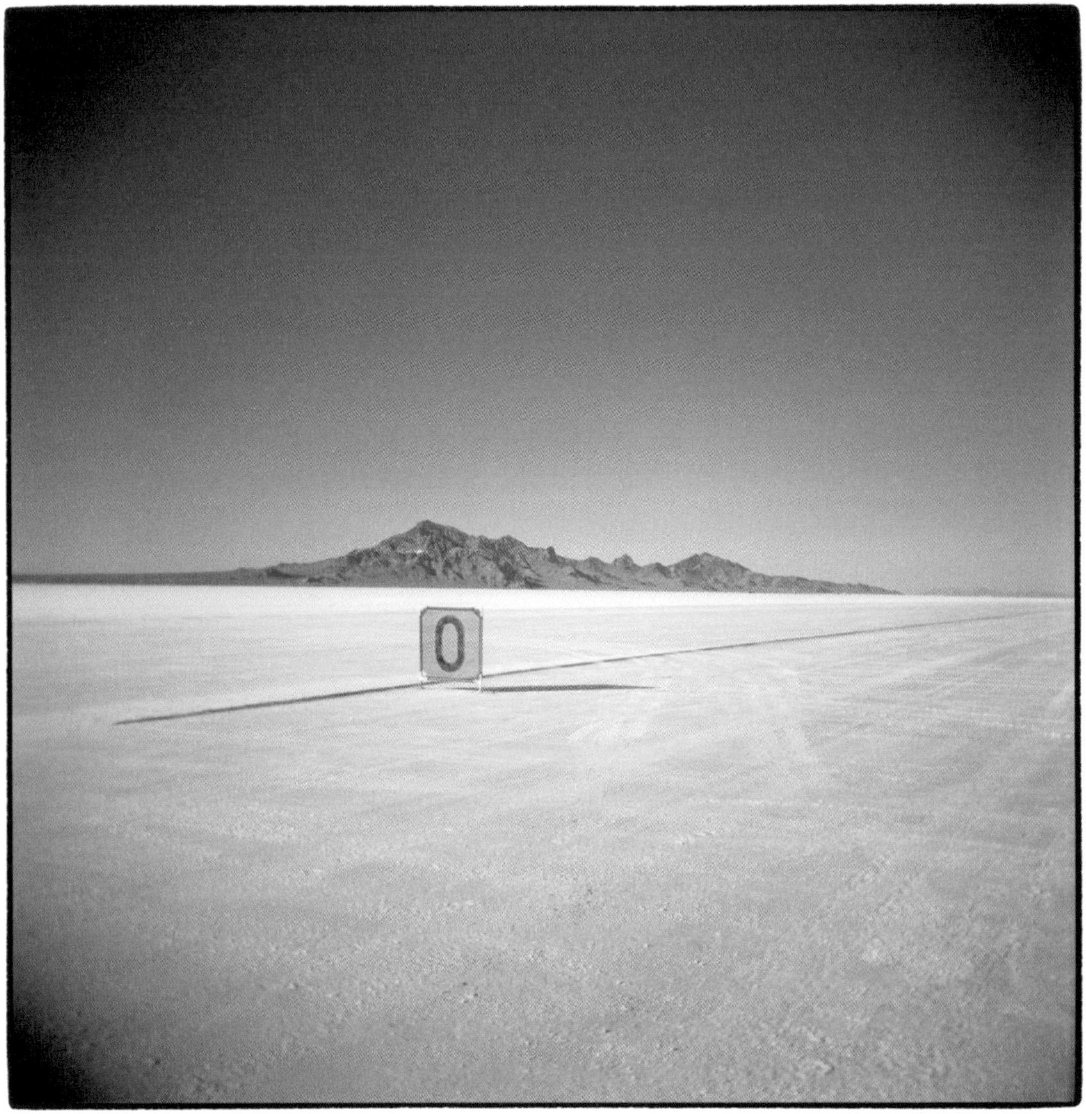
0

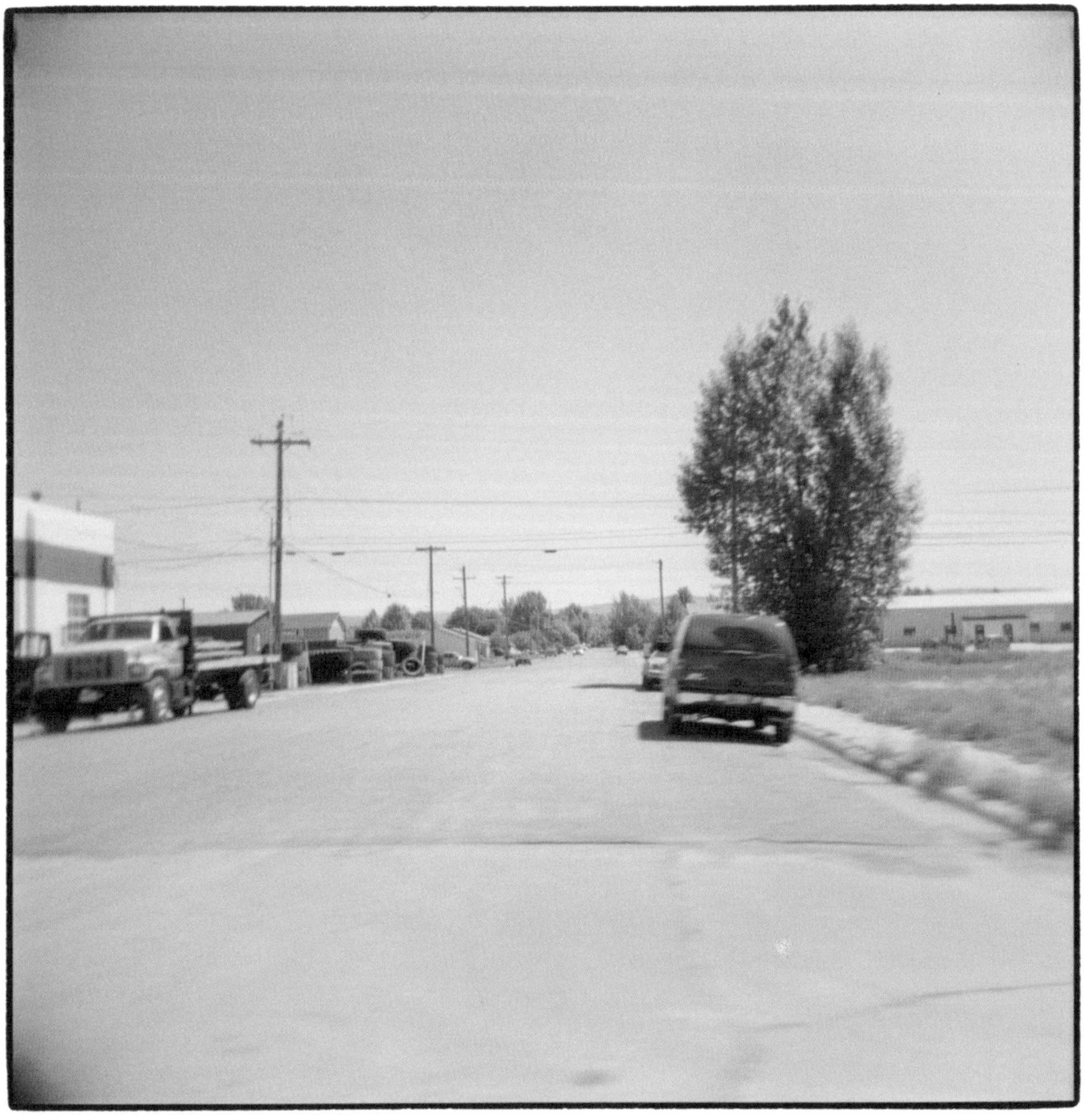

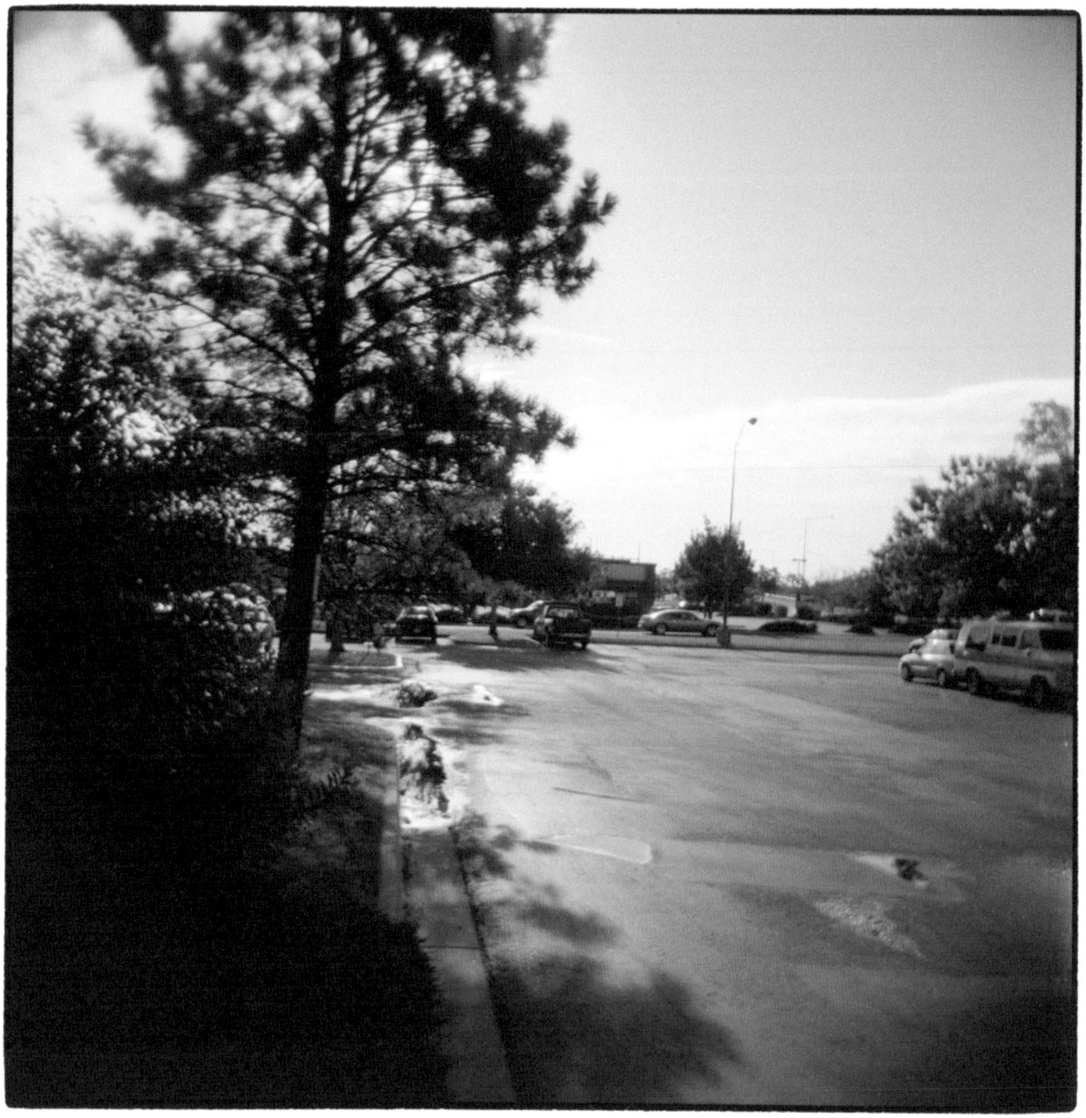

Comfort INN

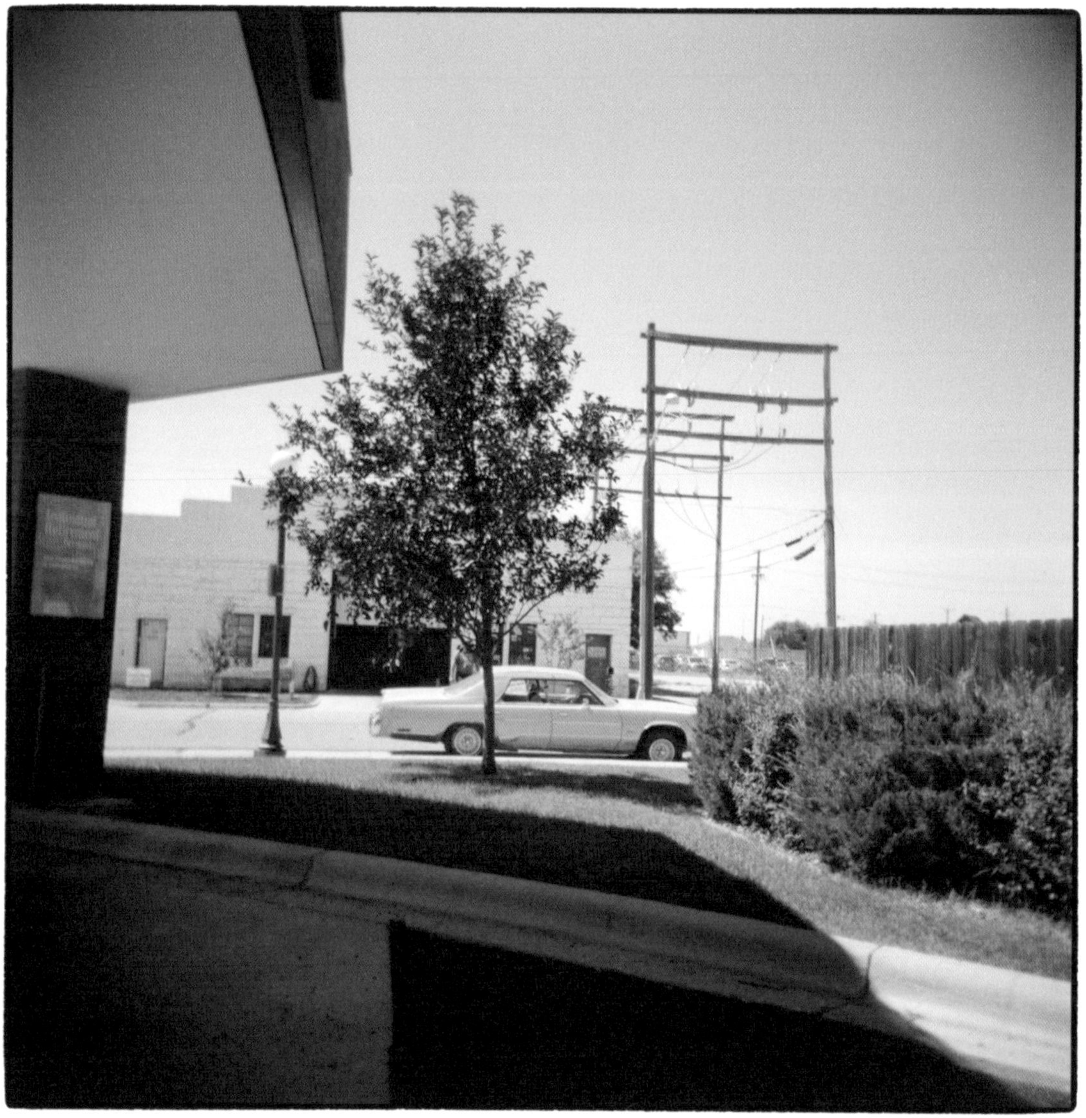

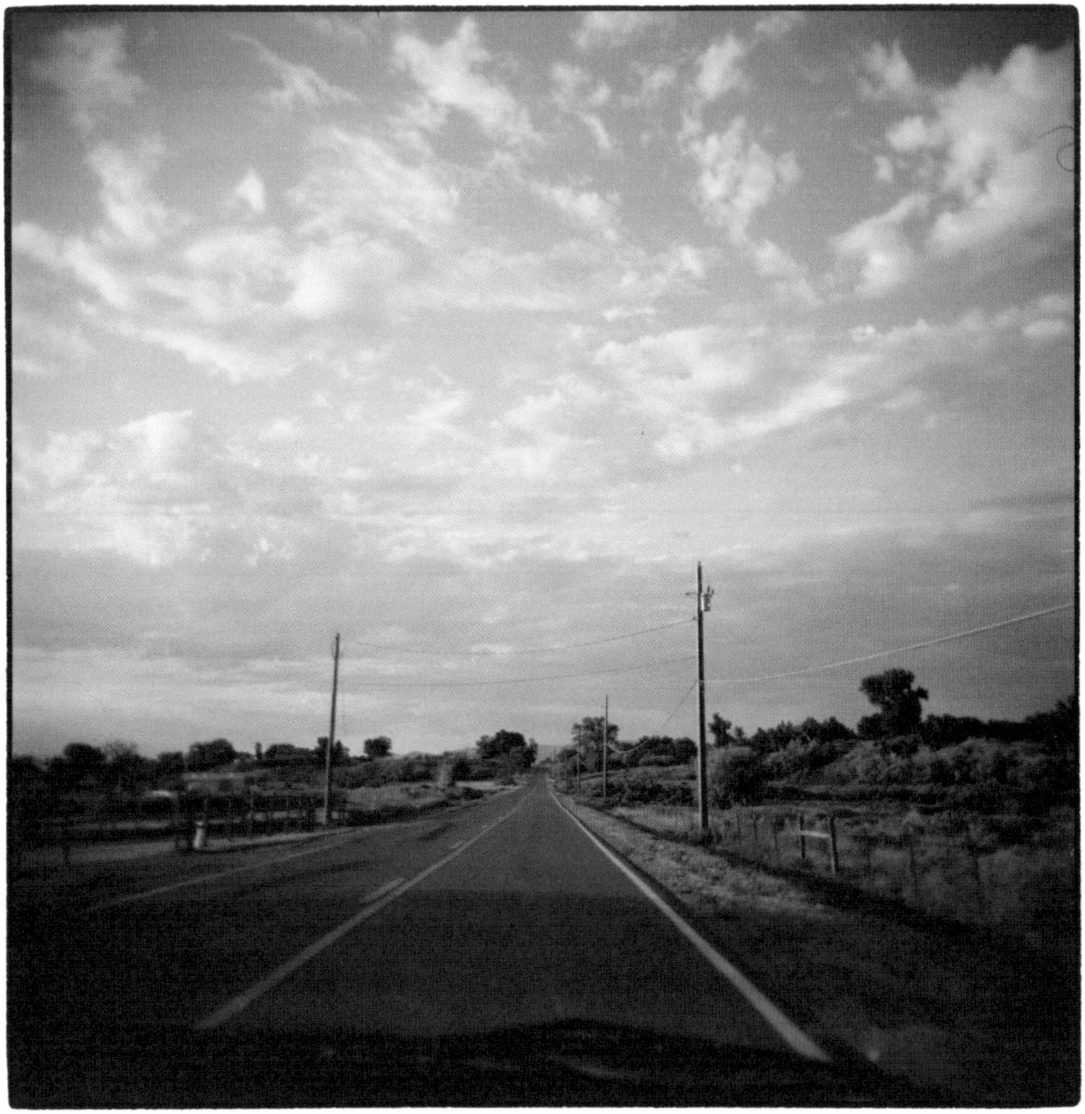

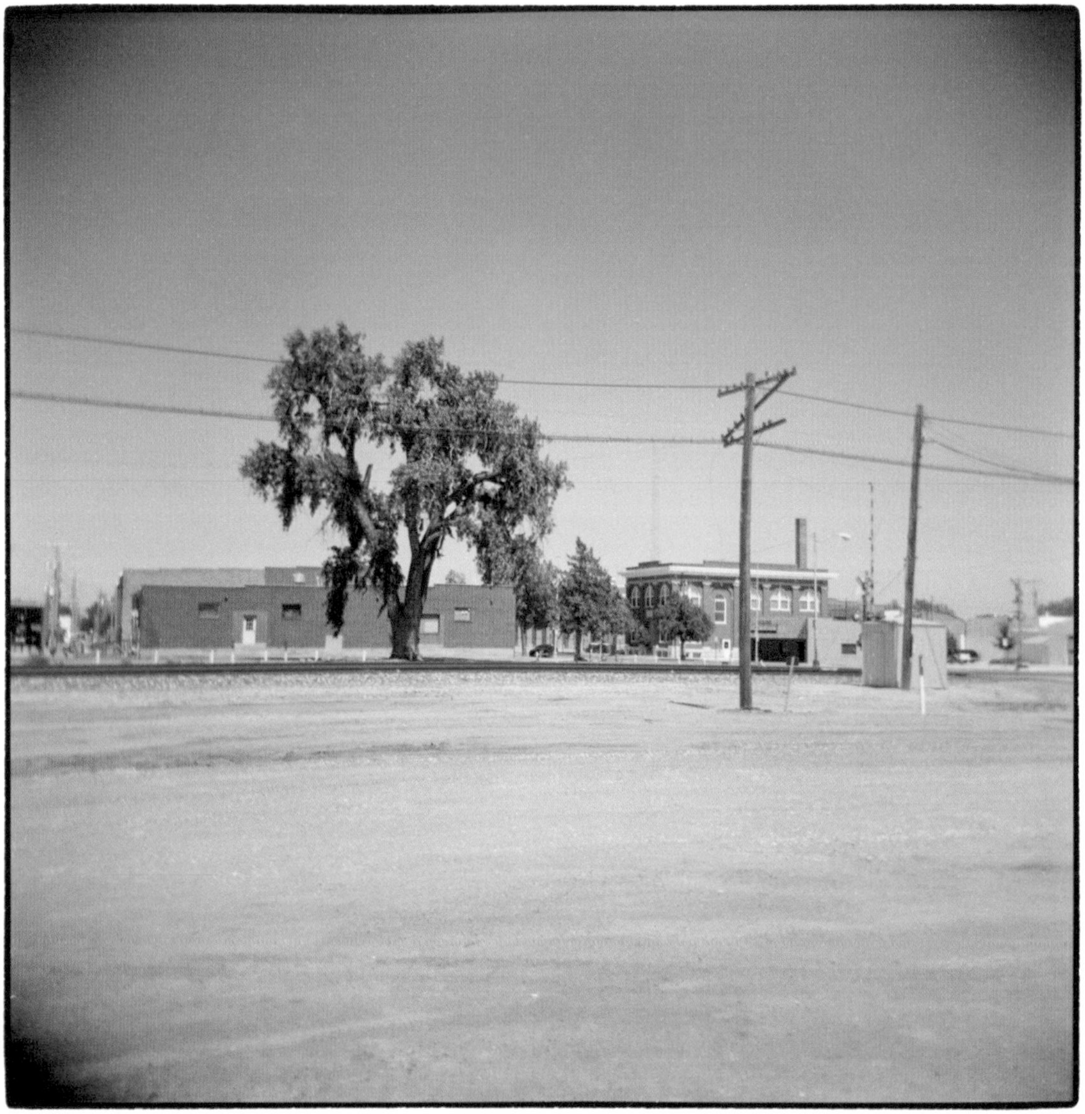

6
Exit 102-Then Left

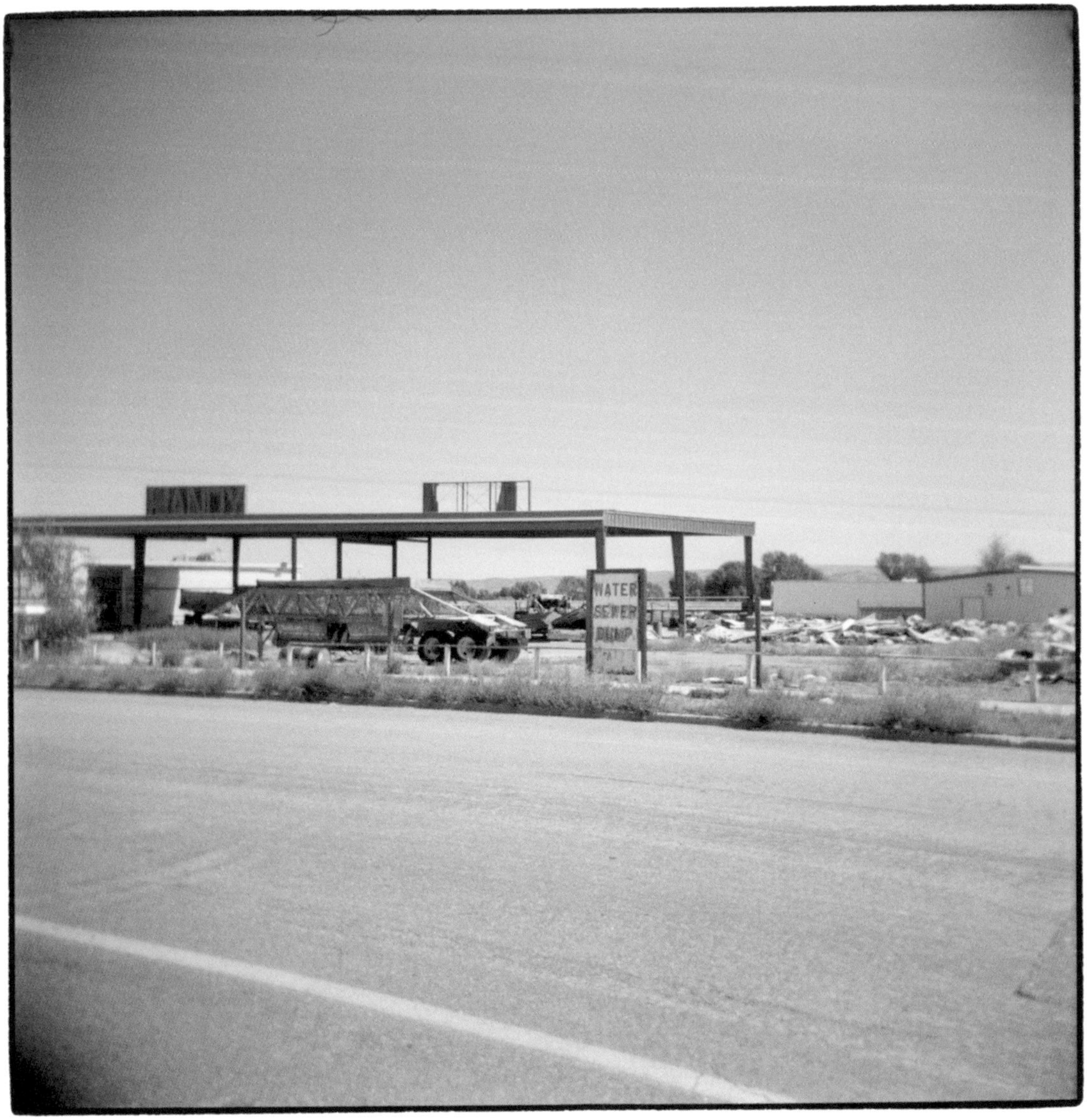
WATER
SEWER
DUMP

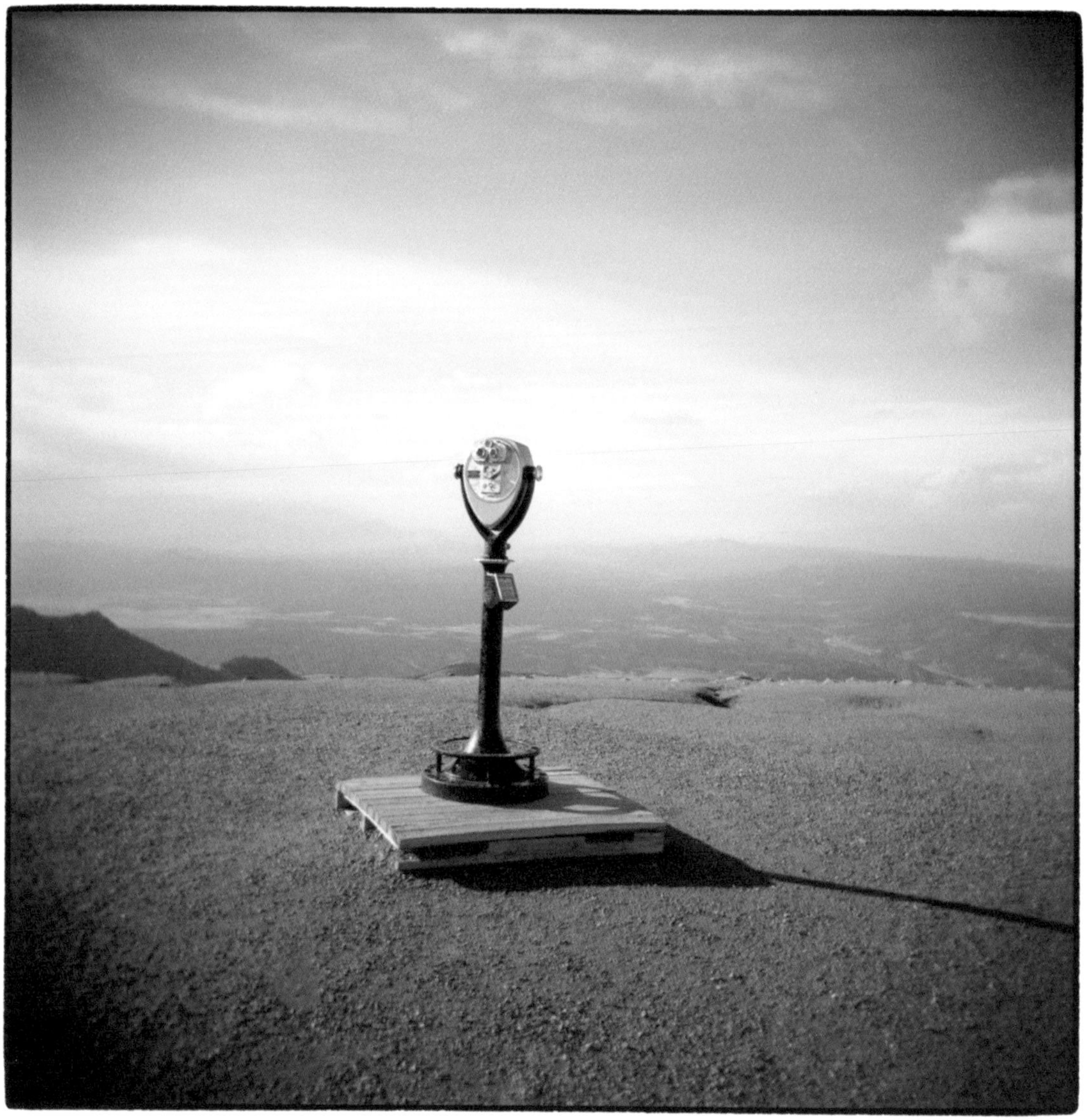

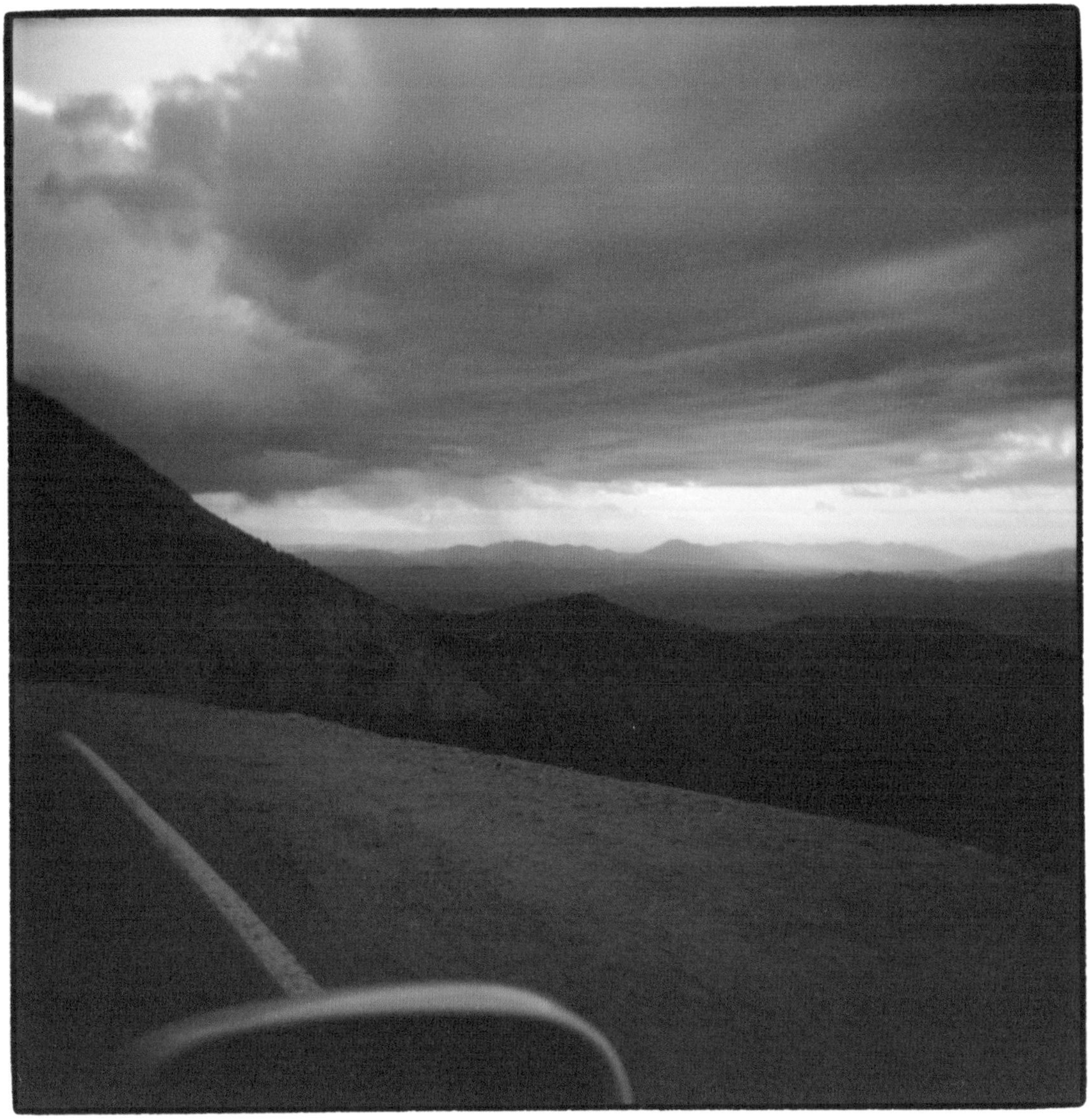

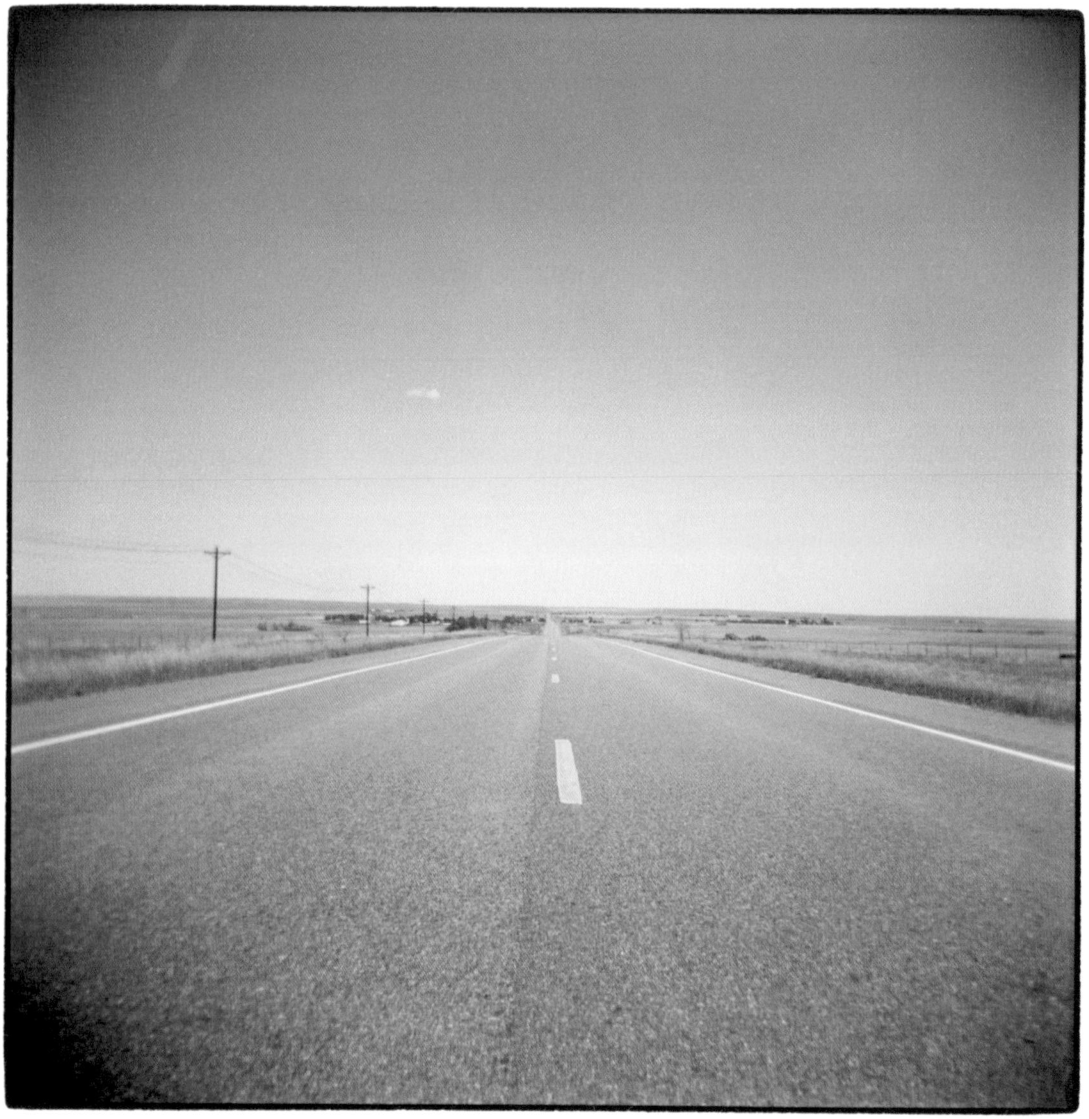

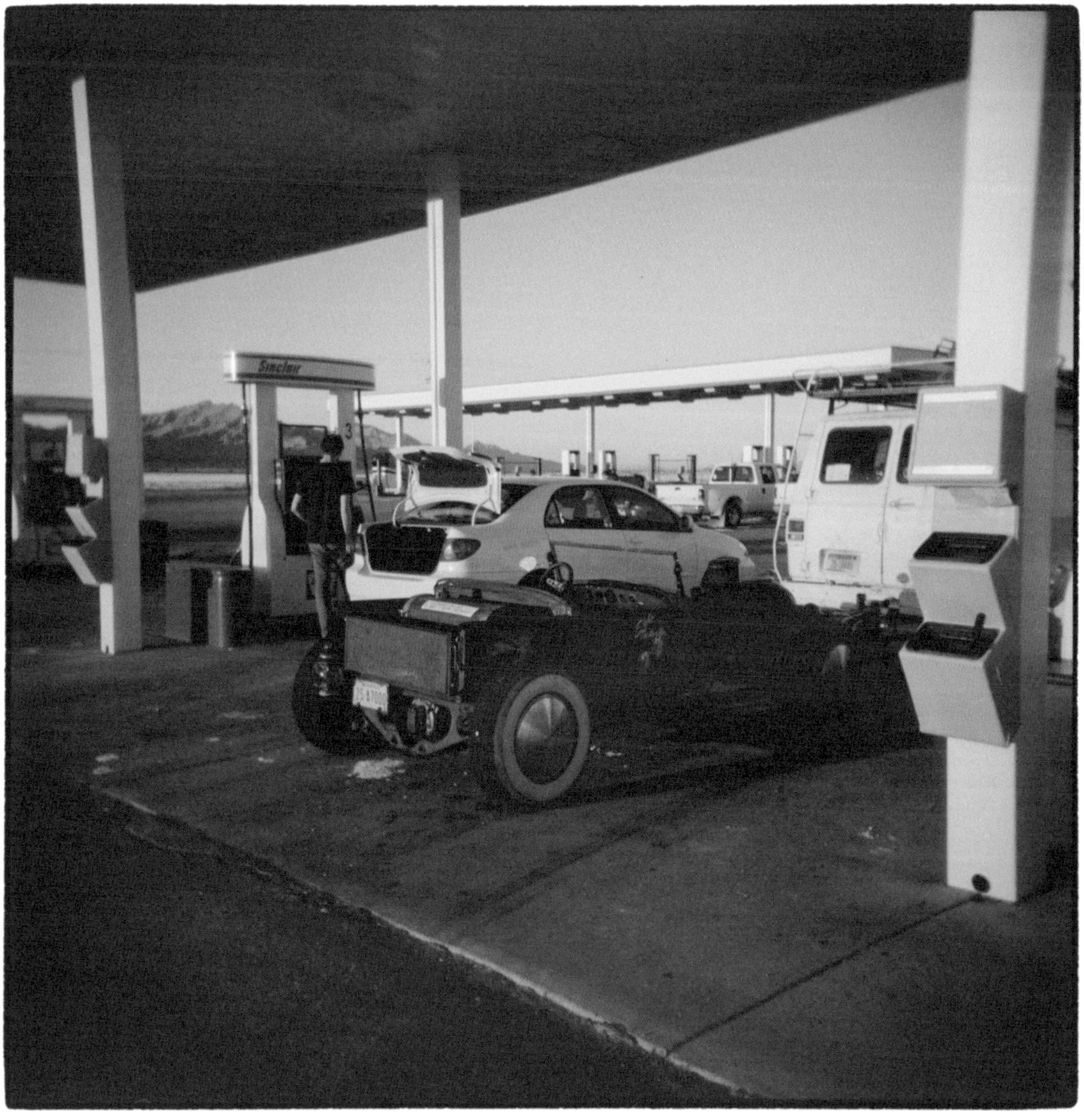
Sinclair

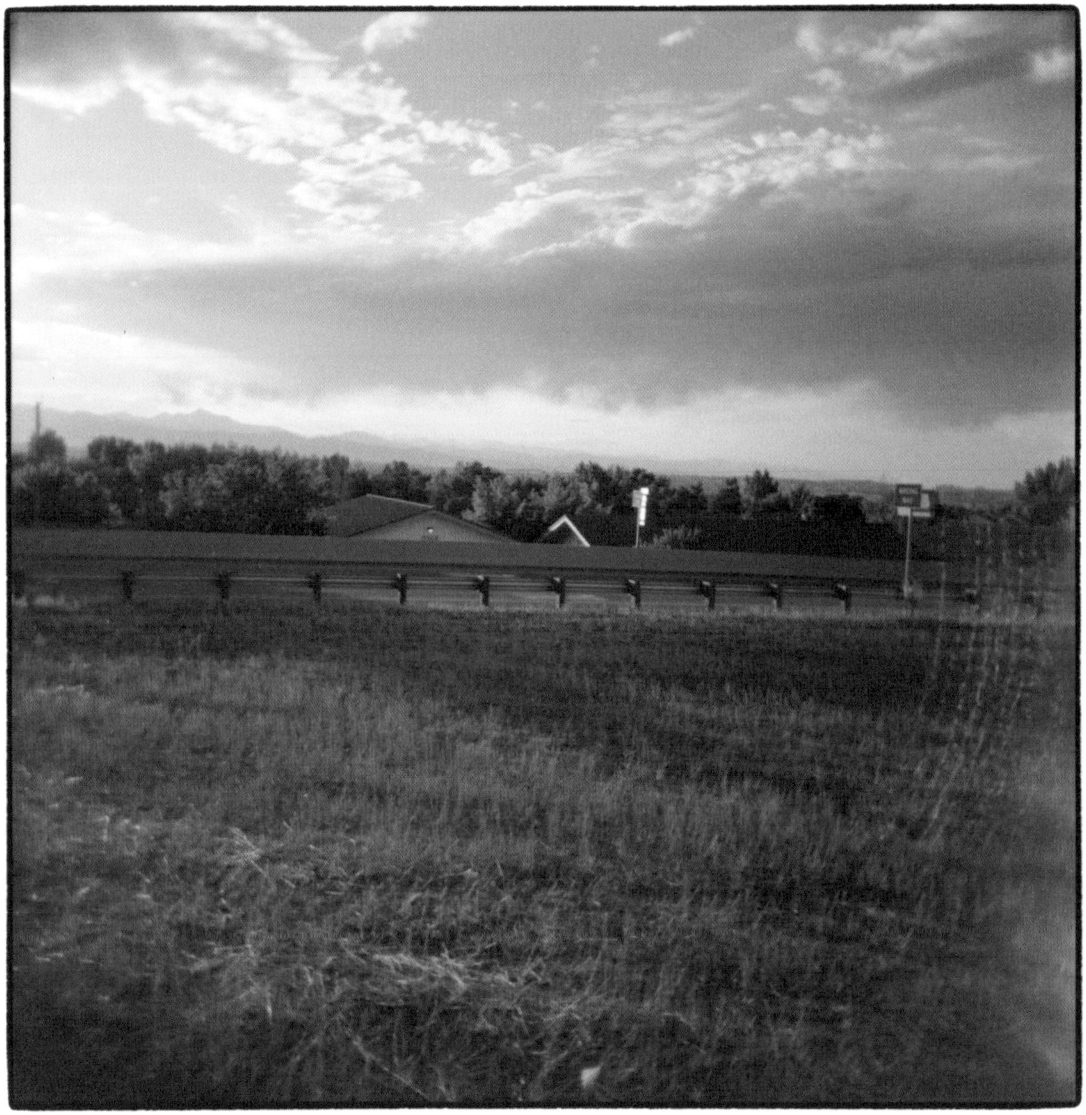

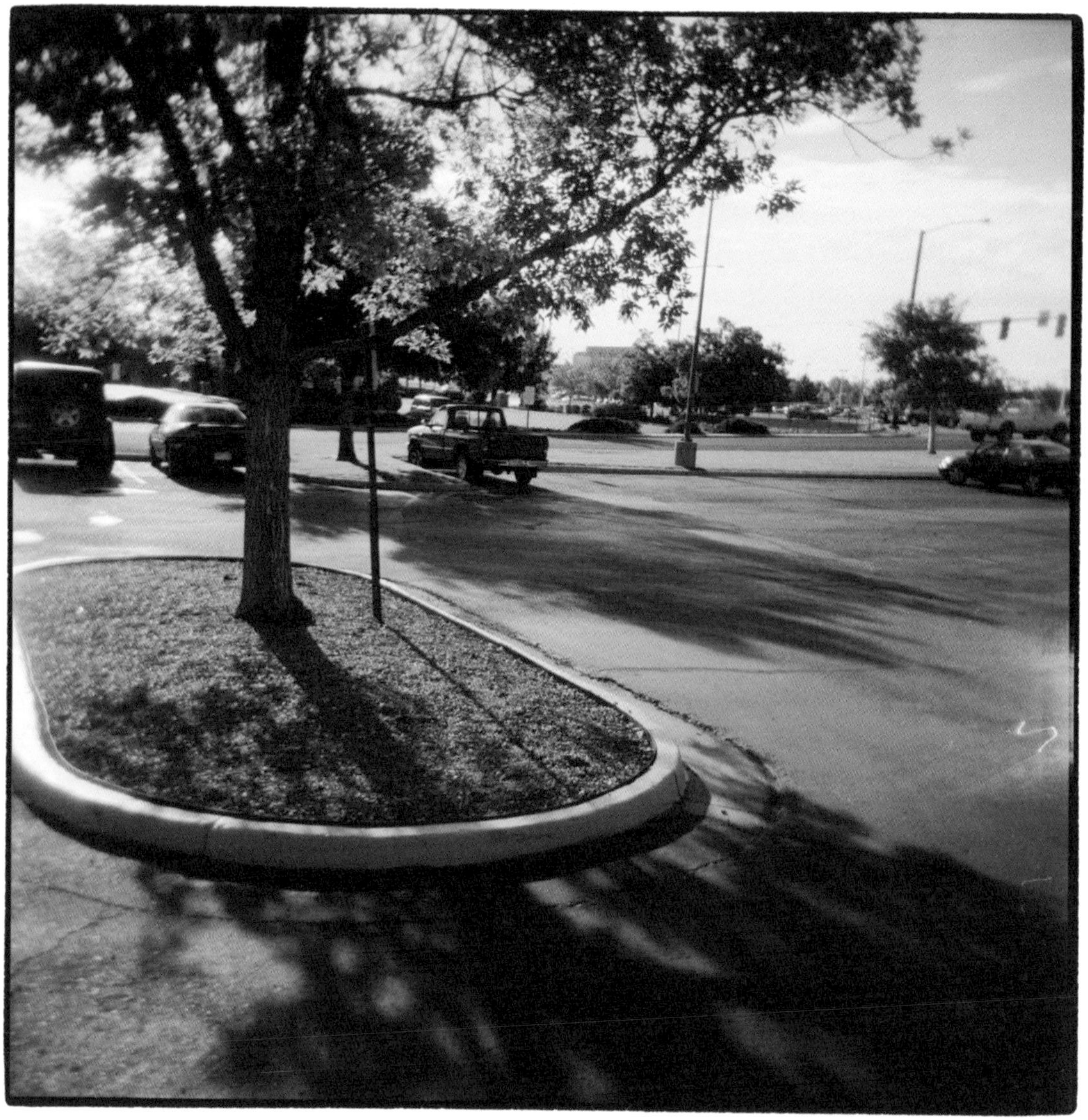

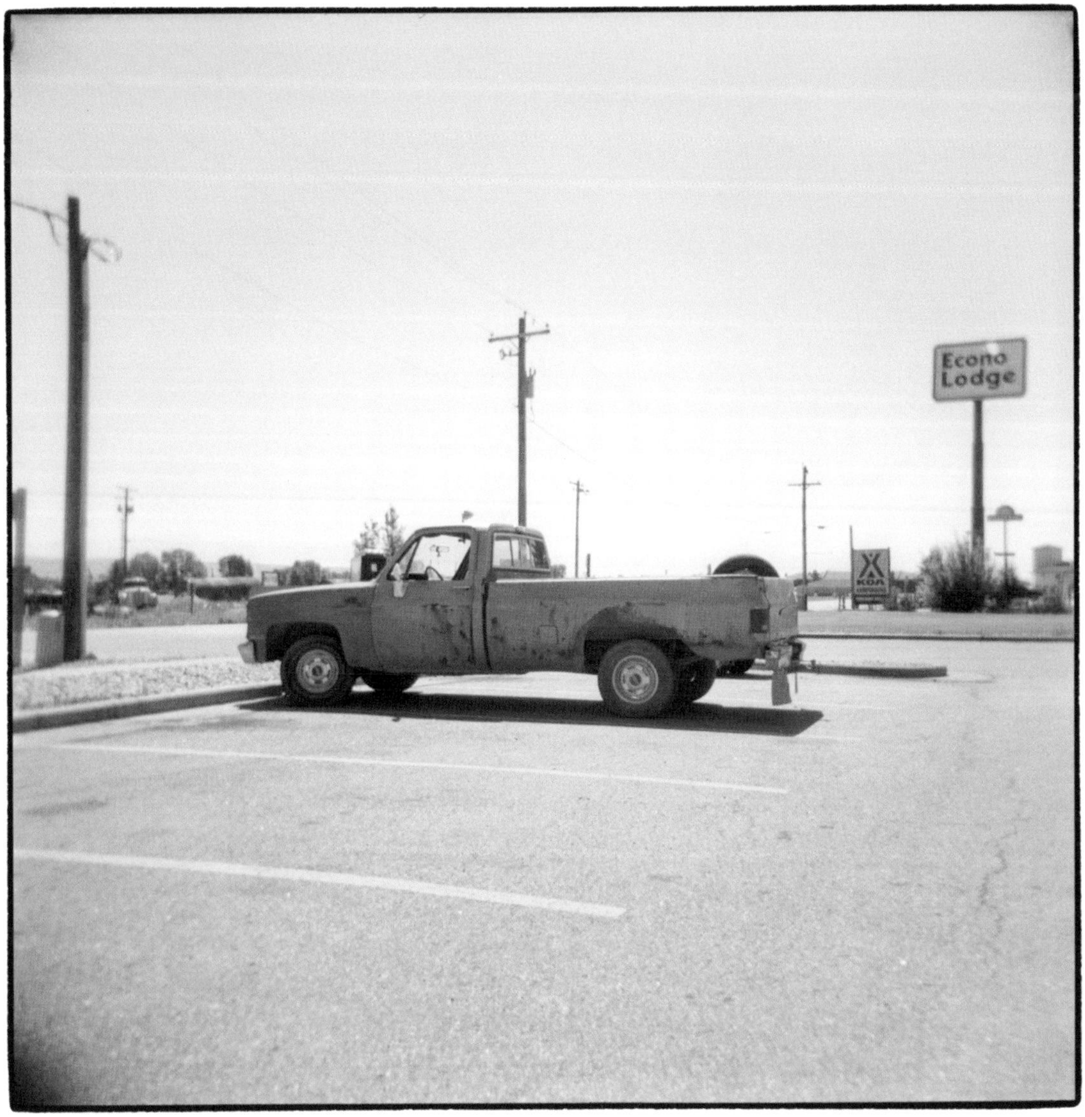
Econo
Lodge
KOA

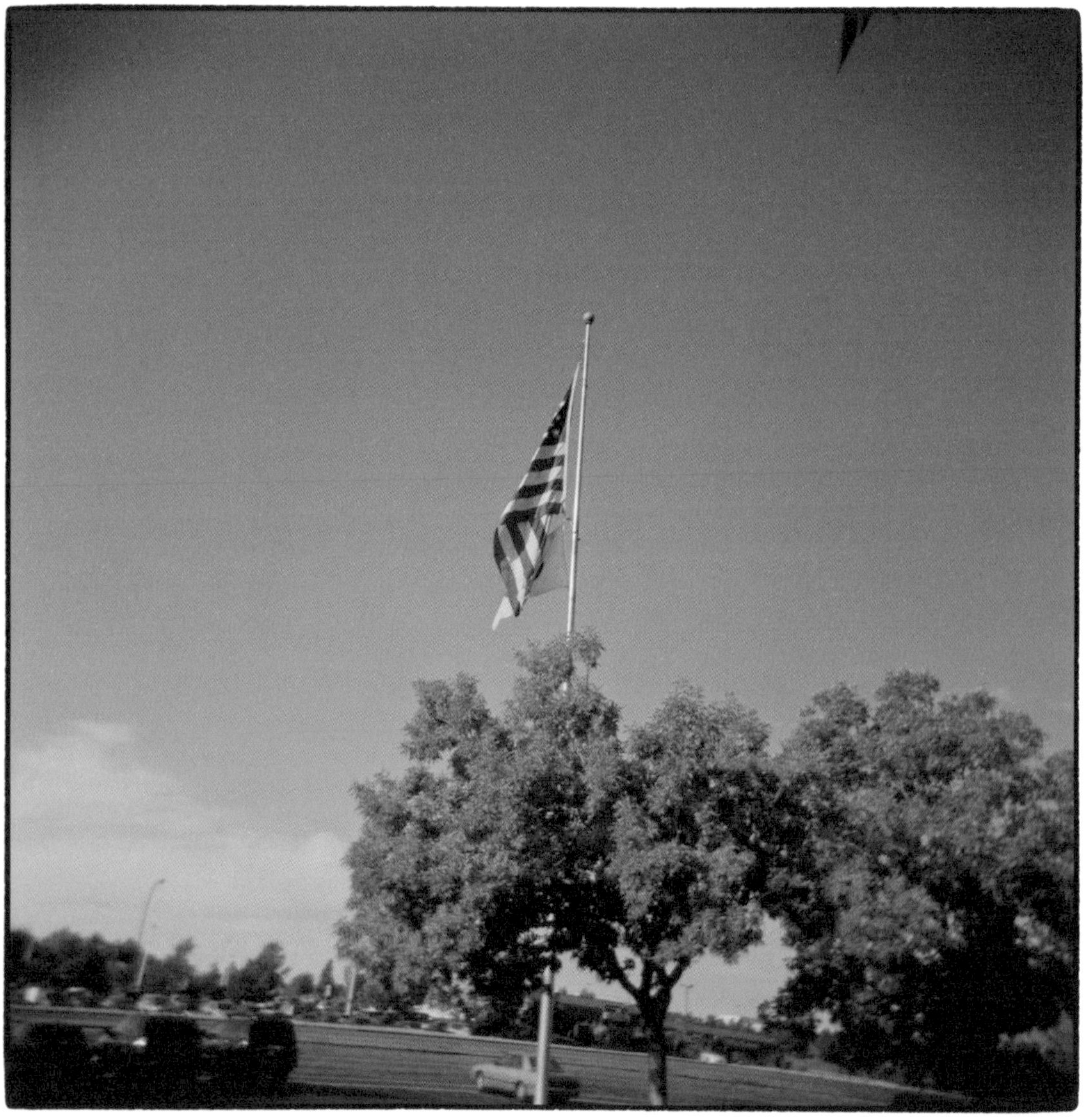

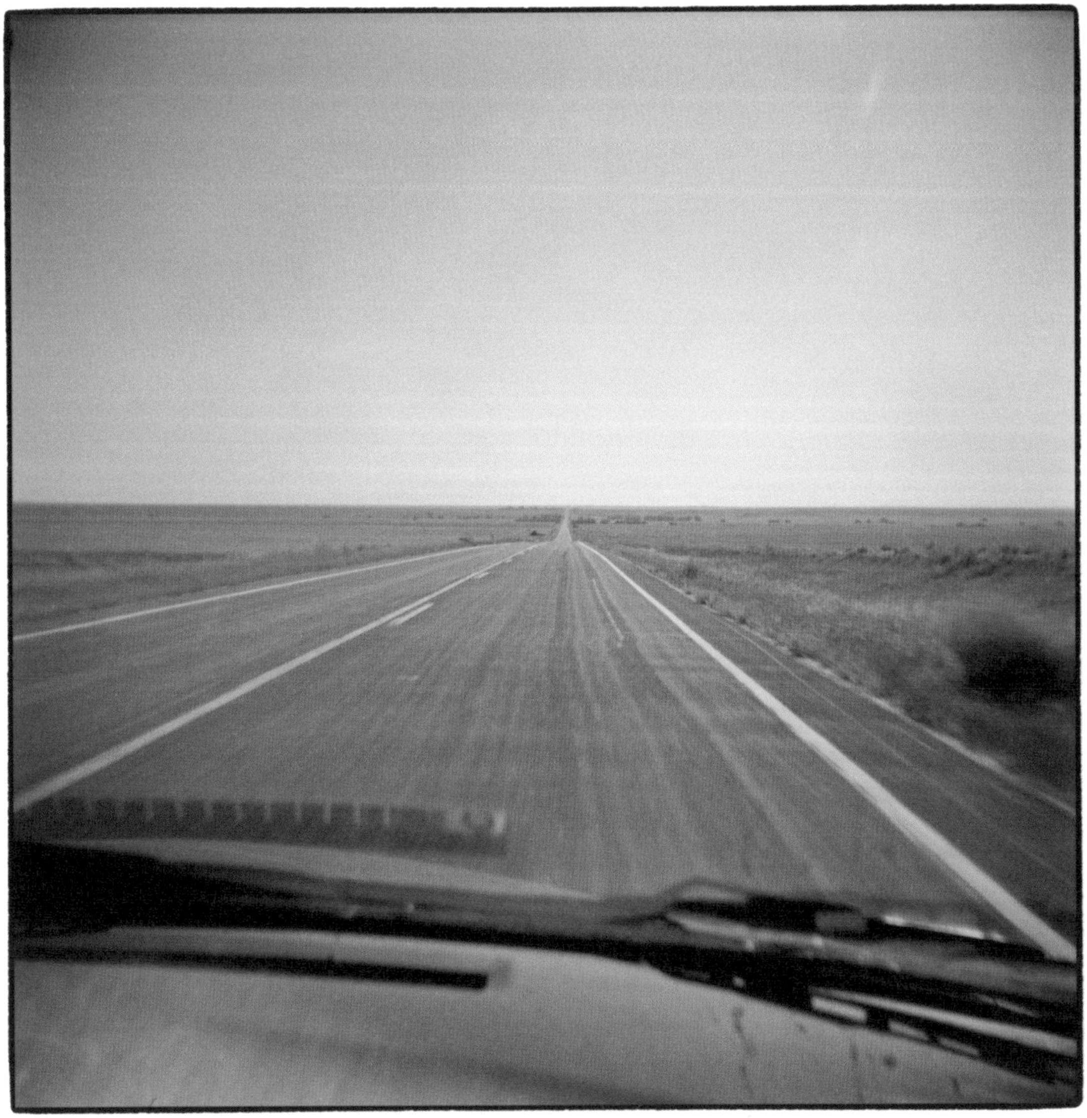

Rich Webster

Sacred Sites

Rich Webster

If you set off on a journey, at some time in the future and by some route you will arrive at your destination. The most important thing is to set off. The unfortunate thing about most journeys we make in the modern high speed era is that there is a tendency to arrive even before you set off. A journey becomes almost an exercise in health and safety techniques where one would assess the weight, clear the route and prepare the ground in order to move from A to B.

In a sense the journey along the Camino, the Santiago de Compostella, as a traditional route, is just this. So traditional, so well trodden and loaded with a feeling of completing another life experience to be logged as another consumable of modern life, is this route, that there is a danger of missing the point.

If you want to go to Santiago, catch a plane. It's easy, relatively cheap; the anxiety of arriving at your destination is short, and you can be there pretty quick, within your schedule, do what you need to do in Santiago and be back home in time for tea.

If you are going on a journey to Santiago de Compostella, you might at some time end up in there, but the journey will decide how and when that will be. It is only when you open up to the possibilities of the journey that you have any say in your destiny. You cannot think of it in terms of then and there. It has to be in terms of here and now, here and now, here and now, experiencing everything within the boundaries of each here and now. That way you really meet the people you meet, taste the wine you drink and the food you eat. But the main point is that you meet yourself and then, as in the Buddhist saying, 'if you meet Buddha on the road, kill him, but not before you have met him'; once you have met yourself you can destroy yourself in order to change yourself.

In a traditional sense the pilgrimage was always a journey to somewhere, usually to visit a sacred place, which in the case of the journey to Santiago, is to visit the shrine where the body of St James is entombed. But the pilgrim of five hundred or a thousand years past would have a different attitude towards this journey than the pilgrims of today. With fewer constraints on their lives and less transport opportunities the pilgrims would start the journey literally by leaving their front door. The modern Camino, while it has a number of starting points, has starting points nonetheless and the journey, by another mode of transport to that point of egress is forgotten.

There is a sense of making the pilgrimage a unit with a start and an end and a certain amount of time to travel from one to the other. This is mostly done by walking; perhaps this is born out of some pseudo-tradition of pilgrim activity. Of course pilgrims of the past would have walked, but not because they wanted to. Traditionally the options for travel were walk or horse, and if you had no horse the options halved. But it is clear that many pilgrims of the 'merchant class' would make the journey under horse power, and if there had been cars, buses, rail or even bicycles, these would also have been used. The way the journey was made was irrelevant as long as the journey was made and it took you to the holy place at the end.

My journey was not to be an agnostic journey. The view I have taken of God is that of a force we are all part of and not a greater being that can only be accessed through religion. My view is therefore all-inclusive whether one believes in God through religion or whether one does not even recognise God, but recognises there might be something in the Force from Star Wars or Elvis or a new car or another person or nature, science and mathematics.

With the tradition of the pilgrimage being present in all major religions, my task was to consider whether it is the proximity of the holy place or the journey which leads to that sense of spiritual wellbeing that pilgrims seek, and if it is the journey, can we derive some spiritual wellbeing from more common journeys like the bus ride to work or the walk to the shops or even the much-feared flight to a holiday destination?

My expectation was that the places, shrines and cathedrals would be impressive but not spiritually uplifting, appreciated more for their aesthetic rather than their significance. Many people I met on this journey were doing it to be in these holy places, but just as many were not, expecting that the journey would satisfy something other than their intellectual and physical being and often making a contemplative or searching journey, contemplating and searching for anything. Perhaps the beginnings of something that would change their life.

In considering the place and the journey as the two spiritual elements to a pilgrimage, I wanted to change the point of view whereby I could assess the values of a 'common' journey to a 'common' place like the supermarket. To this end I identified 16 Lidl supermarkets in some of the major towns through which I was to pass with the intention of—having been guided to the main religious centre by way of scallop shells and yellow arrows—forging a further, 'urban pilgrimage' to the supermarket, thereby affording the possibility of a comparison.

The choice of pilgrimage, from the many pilgrimages around the world, was not arbitrary. Coming from a country largely influenced by Christianity, a Christian route stayed within the realms of my primary experience. But the hook for me came during the research period where I found that the Camino de Santiago was, during the medieval times, known as the Pilgrimage of Everyman, and taking 'Everyman' to mean everyone without consideration of social tagging, the choice was made. It was the Romans, however, who gave the route the name used today: they called it the road under the stars or "La Voje Ladee", which in English is The Milky Way, and in Spanish, "La Camino de Santiago de Compostella". The journey takes the traveller to Santiago where in the cathedral there is to be found a shrine containing the remains of Saint James.

My chosen 'official' starting point was from St Jean de Pied de Port in the French Pyrenees. This 500 mile route to Santiago passes through the major cities and towns of Northern Spain as well as the ever-changing countryside of Navarra, Rioja, Burgos, Palencia, Leon and the provinces of the ancient kingdom of Galicia. It was once a Roman trade route and also a Celtic migratory route, so while it eventually became a main highway for the spread of Christian teaching, institutions and art, it was and still is so much more. The Muslim or Moorish influence on Spanish history, for example, was helped by this route, and this became a factor in my choice, with the world at the moment seeing a division between Muslim and Christian. Historically this part of Spain has also played host to a large Jewish community and in the 13th century became a melting pot of philosophy and culture. It is known that for pilgrims reaching Santiago and visiting the shrine of Saint James in the Middle Ages, it was then obligatory to continue onto the chapel of Nuestra Senora at Finisterre on the Spanish coast. That part of the route may have been a remnant from an earlier journey made by the Celts that had an earlier more mystical provenance than of the Christian church. Perhaps, as the route was so important, the shrine of St James in Santiago was founded as a way of claiming and populating the route as a Christian journey and a trade route through Europe.

It is well known that the Templar Knights were invited by the Castilian King Sancho III to protect the

Santiago Road, establishing their base in Villacazar in about 1157. There is a great deal of evidence that they operated along the route and most likely would have acted as bankers as well as protectors, allowing pilgrims to deposit gold with them at the beginning and be able to pick it up at the end, perhaps even establishing a system of paper money for the journey. The fate of the Templers is not relevant here but the fact that economic systems were created along the route fits with my considerations of the similarities between cathedral and supermarket.

It is apparent that whilst any cathedral was being built, there would be, as well as the religious personnel, craftsmen and apprentices and suppliers of materials and so on, living on the site, perhaps for their whole lives. It follows then that these people, having been paid by the church would have money to spend and a need to be able to buy goods. This would mean that markets would spring up, and then of course taverns, money lenders, blacksmiths and all the other related trades and businesses. According to Georgio Visari in the book Lives of the Artists, Fillipo Brunelleschi, the Italian architect, created undercover kitchens and eating places in the dome of Santa Maria del Fiore while it was being built in order to make the job more efficient. So the function of the church was not just a centre of religion but also a centre of commerce and society not unlike the modern day shopping mall or supermarket.

There are many similarities between the cathedral and the supermarket in contemporary culture, although they exist separately. Essentially they are both selling something. The cathedral is selling a lifestyle but is usually found to be selling products, souvenirs and postcards. The tradition of the sale of Holy relics goes back many centuries. The supermarket sells products of all kinds as expected, but it is not just about the products we buy but from where we bought them. The reason we buy or at least covet one product over another at a shopping mall is to do with advertising. Lidl sells food, but then there is M & S food. The choice of shop and product makes a statement about our lifestyle, and perhaps even dictates our lifestyle.

If there is a product of status that is synonymous with the Camino it is the simple scallop shell. If you carry one of these you are instantly recognised as a pilgrim, and in Spain that is a status that is respected. Better than any club card it can get you into the cheap hostel, get you hospitality from local communities, and while you are given one at the start of the pilgrimage, it is a massive selling souvenir in the gift shops. There are many stories of why the scallop shell is so important, and many relate to the legends surrounding St James.

St James was the brother of John and both were of the twelve disciples of Jesus. After Jesus had died, the disciples travelled the world spreading the gospel of Jesus. St James spent many years on the Iberian Peninsula; however, he was killed for his convictions in Jerusalem. His body was sent back to the area where he had spent much of his ministry and was first buried in the City of Iria Flavia but later moved to the cathedral in Santiago.

It is said that as the ship carrying his body home approached the shore it had lost its sail and was adrift in rough sea. On the shore a wedding celebration was going on, and as the groom arrived on horseback, he saw the distress of the boat and without even knowing the importance of the boat rode his horse into the sea in an attempt to help the vessel. Both horse and rider disappeared under the waves and the frantic guests searched in vain. After some time the wedding party had given up hope. But as the sea calmed and the boat arrived safely at the shore, the groom emerged from the sea on the horse, and they were covered in scallops, which it is said, saved the groom from drowning. Another story says that the ship was wrecked in a storm, but some days later the body of St James was washed ashore covered in scallops.

There may have been a more practical use for the scallop shell in that it could be used for eating and drinking, or perhaps, as medieval writings show, as the pilgrimage to Santiago became more renowned, a custom grew up of returning from the journey with a Galician scallop shell as proof of completion.

The scallop shell is now a major symbol and souvenir of this pilgrimage, along with postcards, books of the art and artefacts from the various cathedrals, models and crosses and various little comedy mascots, all of which are part of the economy surrounding the cathedrals and pilgrimage as a whole. But this is nothing new. The pilgrim in the Middle Ages would be on the lookout for religious artefacts and relics, the possession of which would have some spiritual significance and be a symbol of a direct relationship to God. Although often fake and sold in great numbers, the pieces of the cross of Jesus and rags from his shroud held for the pilgrim a spiritual power. While the modern pilgrim will have a better general understanding of commercialism, it is clear that these modern mass-produced relics hold some sort of power or significance for the person who owns them.

Extending this thought into modern everyday life, it can be seen how the shopping mall or the supermarket becomes a sacred place where objects can be bought that in some small way add to our salvation, not in the next life but in this one. The objects we buy are part of our spiritual nourishment and make the problems of the world and our immediate lives more bearable. They are not however 'relics' in the traditional sense but are nonetheless surrounded by myth, through the advertising that brings them to our attention. Most of this is based around a perceived lifestyle to be had by having this product. Expensive things of course show an indication of wealth, but cheaper things that are perceived to be expensive are just as good. All these things are 'new relics' which might show that there is contentment with contemporary life in western culture that did not exist in the medieval era where there was a constant expectation of Hell and damnation.

So the pilgrim journeyed in order to pay the prescribed respect out of duty, out of love, out of fear or out of a drive toward self-improvement or superiority, but always as a means of averting the daily grind and of going on a journey. The journey became synonymous with an abdication of the past and a shift towards the new and the future.

In many ways this is still the case. We search out the new and exciting in the products we buy, and the new and exciting places from which to buy them. Often this is the same place but made exciting and influenced by different store layouts. Our journey to the shops is invariably to look for something new. The visiting of the cathedral, the acquisition of icons and the proximity to much worshipped entities allow the believer a spiritual experience in the physical world in a similar way. In the broader sense of the term and going beyond religious belief, spirituality and things spiritual can be accessed by all as a part of the human condition as an 'other' from the physical and intellectual world.

The journey may give a heightened experience of the physical and intellectual outcomes of going to the cathedral or supermarket. The journey heightens the expectation, commits each of us to doing work to achieve our goal of the sacred place and causes us some degree of suffering or sacrifice in order to be there.

The element of visiting our sacred sites that is in our control but different for each of us is the journey. On the Camino de Santiago, we are told and often reminded that it is our journey, which means that while the direction, the route and the destination are very similar or the same for all, the how and why of the journey makes it personal to each. One might run the London marathon to get the best time or one might run the London marathon in a clown suit for other reasons. That said, many people then set off with specific agendas, timetables, aims and beliefs and forget to open up to the expedition, making it a means to an end as so many journeys are. They essentially make someone else's journey. This may be the journey of their fellow travellers, but mostly it is the expected journey as set out by tradition and is true whether travelling to a cathedral or a supermarket, a 500 mile pilgrimage or a bus trip to the shops. When we arrive in a cathedral or a supermarket, we are subconsciously led in a certain direction around the space, to see certain things and not others, and ultimately to be lead to the most important thing, be it the tomb of St James or the special offers. We fall into these traps very easily, because we are conditioned to be creatures of habit. This is not a bad thing in the physical world, but with the spiritual, we have to make our own rules and lose our conditioning. I think unless you set off on this with the purpose of one foot in front of the other and so on, you are not open to finding the answers you seek. If you have planned the journey then you will have planned it the same way you live your life, and a life that is planned is a life that is closed. The opportunity presented by a journey is to make change.

I met far too many people who had arranged some time off work, a month or 5 weeks in order to 'do' the Camino. And too many were up at 4 a.m., walked 50k each day and missed everything. 'I wish I had met more Spanish people' one girl said to me on the last night before Santiago. She was in bed by 10 and up at 4 and fretting that she would not get to Santiago before all the accommodation was filled because of the festival.

Meeting this girl, it struck me that we had set off on this journey with no real plan. We always found accommodation, an obsession with many of the other pilgrims we met: we had been in Pamplona when the bull running was on; we had been to a young priest's mass in Obanos; several times we had found water and food just as we had run out and at the point of meeting this girl we were about to be in Santiago for the festival—something for which she had planned but which had just happened to us. She simply seemed to be following her plan and not making her journey.

Conversely we walked for a few miles to the town of Logrono with a man called Paulo. He spoke little English but had been learning for a year. He had had four heart operations and now had a new life. He was only walking for the day, but he was walking the whole Camino at weekends and holidays and odd days here and there. He was not very old and worked as a part time Quantity Surveyor because of the heart problems, but he was in no hurry to finish the journey, even though his health might stop him at any time. Because he knew this, he enjoyed the journey and not the outcome. Everything he saw and smelt and tasted was in each step he made.

People get so wrapped up in the expected journey—the planned journey—that they forget to make choices. The problem is that we cease to desire the unique or to be unique and can only find our identity through uniformity.

The enhancement of the spirit is a personal thing. It is a development of one's self. This would seem to be a selfish act. But, the true development of one's self should lead to a state of love that expands to the people around that self, adding to their development and generally a better state of being.

We have this outdated model of development and teaching that tries to develop en masse. Big organisations with a pyramid structure of management make policy for all their employees rather than for individuals, and then their teams of people. In all cases the policy is made for the lowest common denominator. The slow learners at school are given the highest attention while the fast learners are held back and not allowed to develop at their natural pace. The option and encouragement to excel is quashed by a pseudo-socialist concern for the mass of people.

There is a fear of developing the individual, perhaps, because of reasons of social control, where a mass is easier to control than a mass of individuals. There is a fear of even being the individual perhaps born out of a need for security of the group. A greater reliance on a group means a diminishing in the common social responsibility where it becomes all too easy to relinquish our responsibilities to others.

Part of the point of going to the Lidls was to take us to places we would not normally have seen, real Spain if you like: a place where we experienced a sense of family and community where essentially modernist living works. The good weather may play a big part in this, but I developed a view of Spain where people realise that essentially people do not need too much of the material and by favouring a strong social ethic, most needs can be shared. That is why public transport works, that is why high-rise living works and why the public gardens are well kept and full of people of all ages. There is a sense of ownership that benefits all and not shareholders. It was good to see extended families out together, with teenage boys playing with the small children and the small children entertaining their grandparents. In the U.K. someone would be prosecuted for something in this scenario.

'You are the culture. Not the Cathedrals not the Monuments' was a part of a poem I saw on a cement works wall near Navarra. We found that our 'Urban Pilgrimages' could not always be planned by using the local tourist maps, and while they would give us a general direction, we often had to ask for directions; we often got lost, and we often took long lunches in cafes or picnics in parks having strayed from the most convenient path, not knowing that our destination was just round the next bend. All of this added to the excitement of catching sight of the red, yellow and blue signs, the roundel within a square that is the Lidl sign, a sign that was so familiar, even commonplace, but that now marked the site of a new discovery, a new sacred place and the achievement of our goal. One day we walked about 13km and decided that shopping is good for you, because you can potentially walk a long way. People should be encouraged to walk further when they shop, to get off the main drag and go to smaller shops that are often part of a community and not just part of big business, where you can buy something special and different.

So we made our journey and collected our sacred relics, not models of cathedrals or images of saints but a series of photos of Lidl supermarkets. In keeping with the journey of 'Everyman' we took only mobile phones and one old digital camera: a Sony Ericsson W810, a Sony Ericsson W 890i and a Sony Cyber Shot camera, all high tech but low resolution, disposable and snatching ephemeral relics of our journey. More than ever, through our ability to manipulate images, these relics can be given new meanings and mystical significance.

On arriving in Santiago, we found we were quite close to the cathedral and consequently the pilgrim office nearby. This is the official end of the journey where, subject to the presentation of a suitably stamped Camino Passport, we could have been issued with a certificate to show that we had made the journey. But we deliberated as to whether we should do this, as we had not bought into the obsession of stamping the passports and had not really kept to the official route. But in the spirit of having a full experience, we queued on the 19 steps of the old building for about an hour to get into an office with 5 or 6 desks, where volunteers would give you the final stamp and certificate.

We had been told by another pilgrim that you had to have walked the last 100km to qualify for a certificate. As we had only walked 40 of the last 100, we hoped that this was not the case. We had walked at least 400miles plus our own urban pilgrimages, so surely we would qualify. But what if you had walked 450miles and then got a bus for the last 50 miles, to get to the festival maybe, would you qualify?

Alas the pilgrim spoke the truth. But this was not, for us, about getting a piece of paper at the end of it. We left, a little down and annoyed at the prescribed system but glad we had realised that we had made our own journeys and not that of someone else.

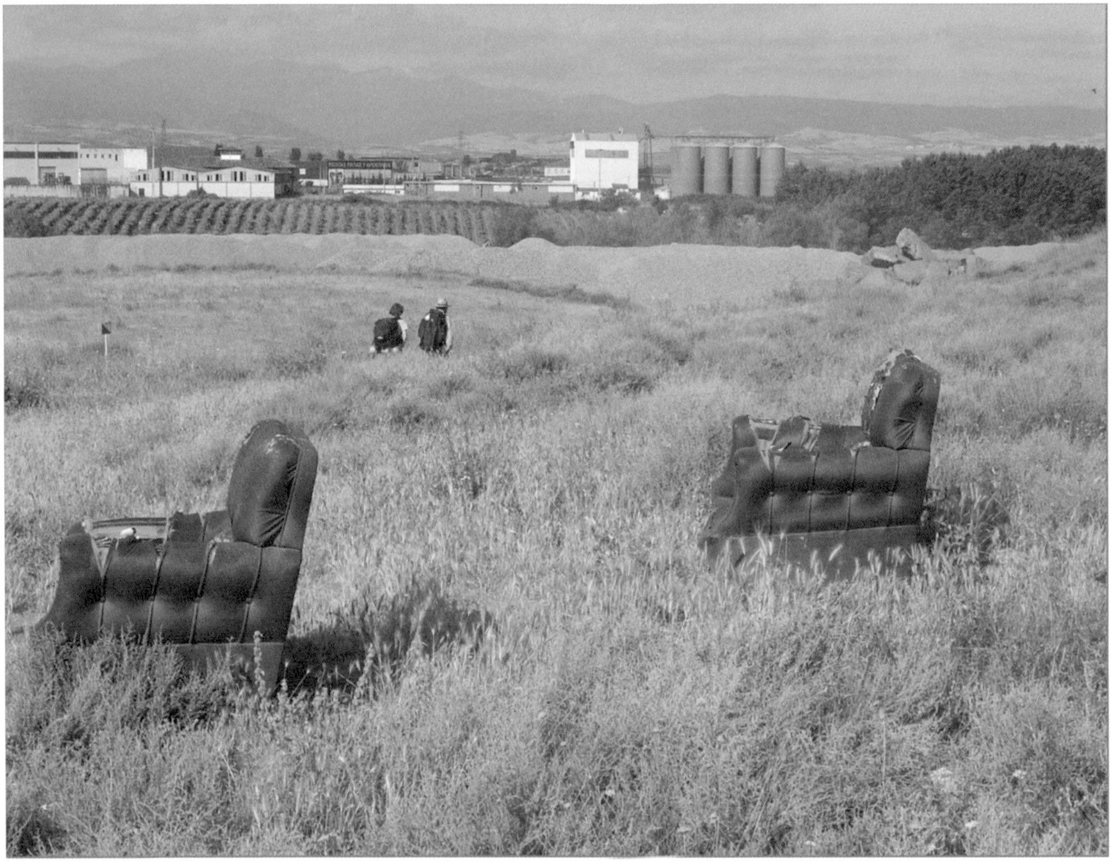

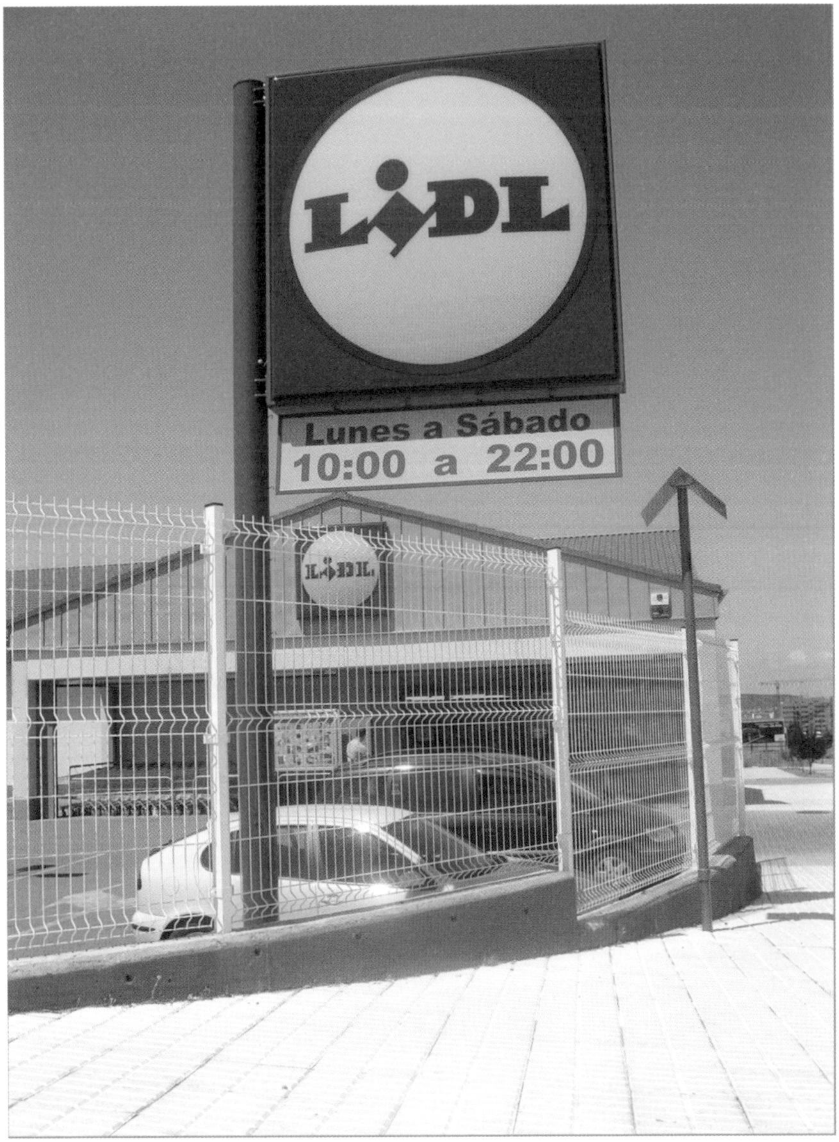
LiDL
Lunes a Sábado
10:00 a 22:00
LiDL

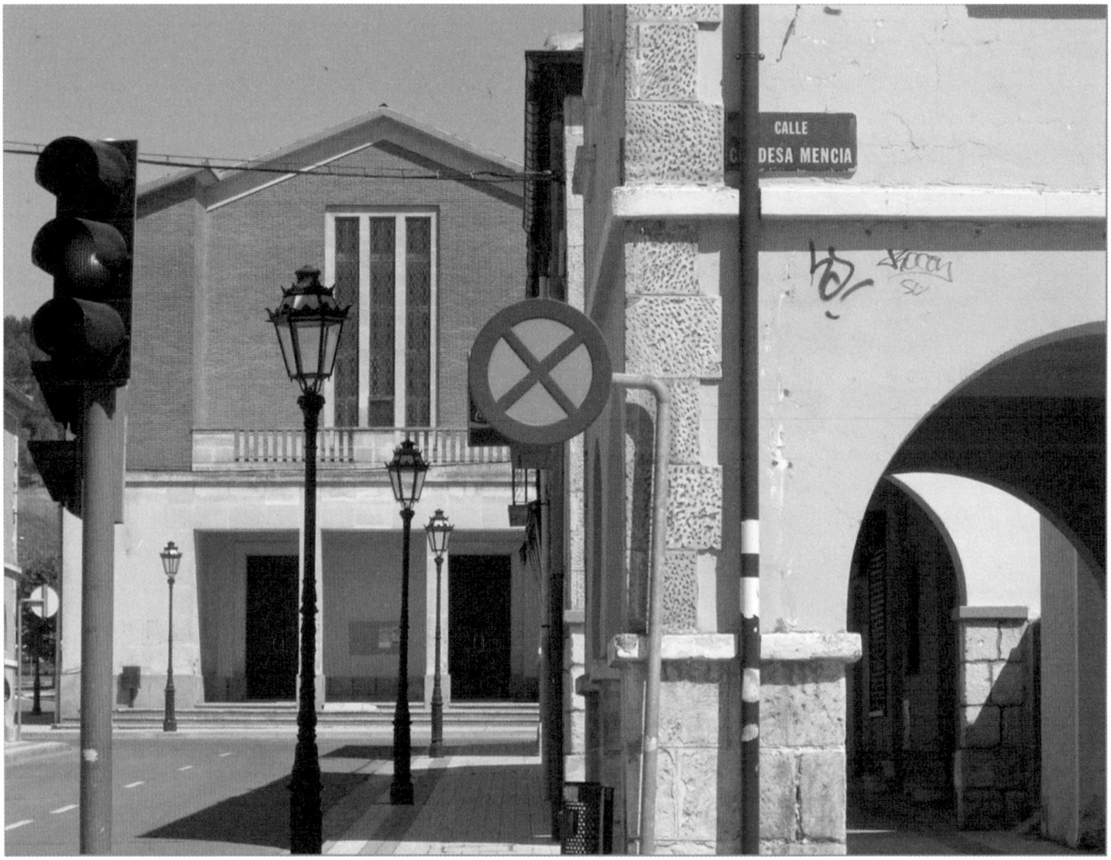
CALLE
DESA MENCIA

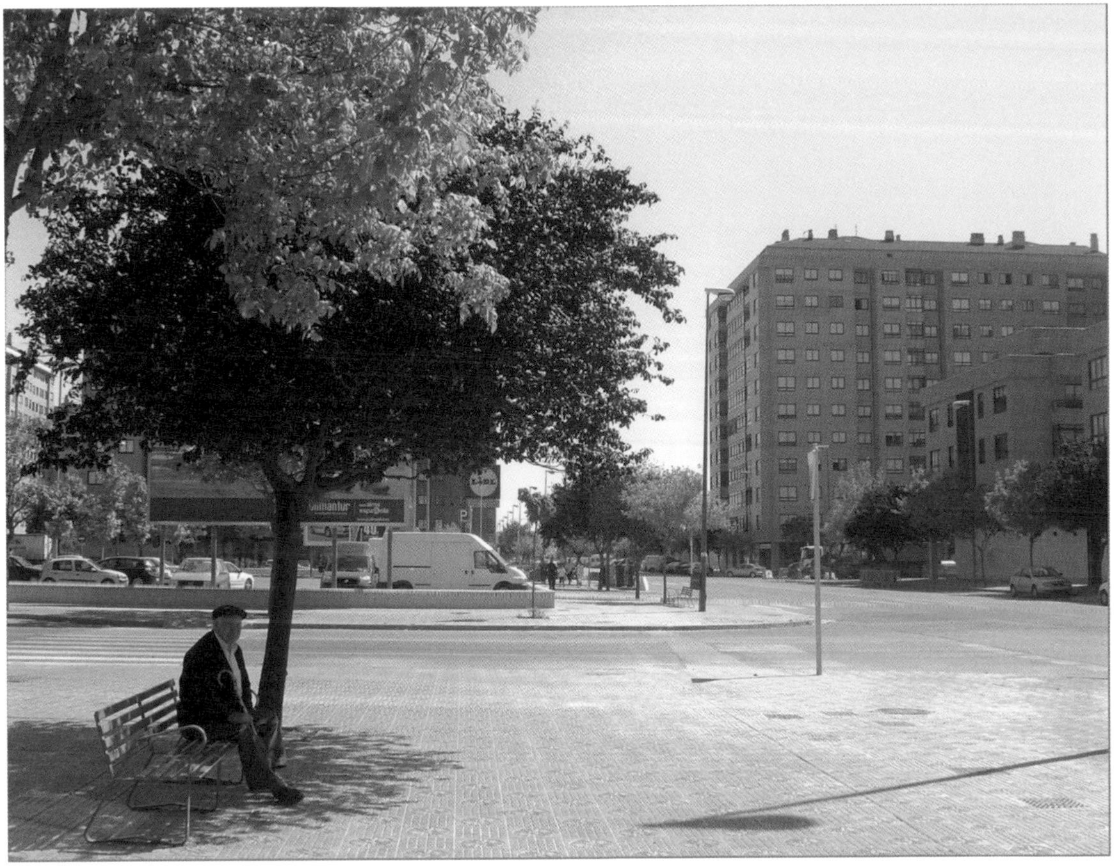

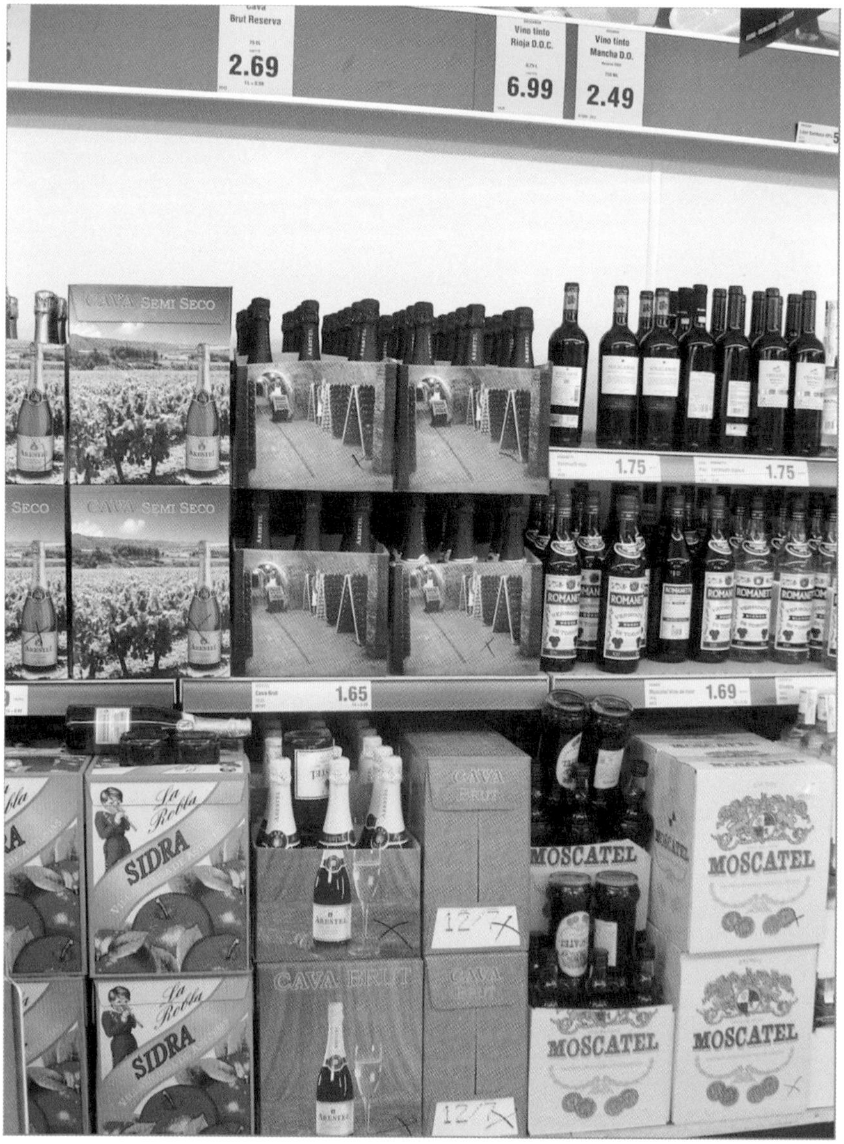
Cava
Brut Reserva
2.69
Vino tinto
Rioja D.O.C.
6.99
Vino tinto
Mancha D.O.
2.49
CAVA SEMI SECO
CAVA SEMI SECO
1.75
1.75
Cava Brut
1.65
1.69
La Robla
SIDRA
La Robla
SIDRA
CAVA BRUT
CAVA BRUT
CAVA BRUT
MOSCATEL
MOSCATEL
MOSCATEL
MOSCATEL

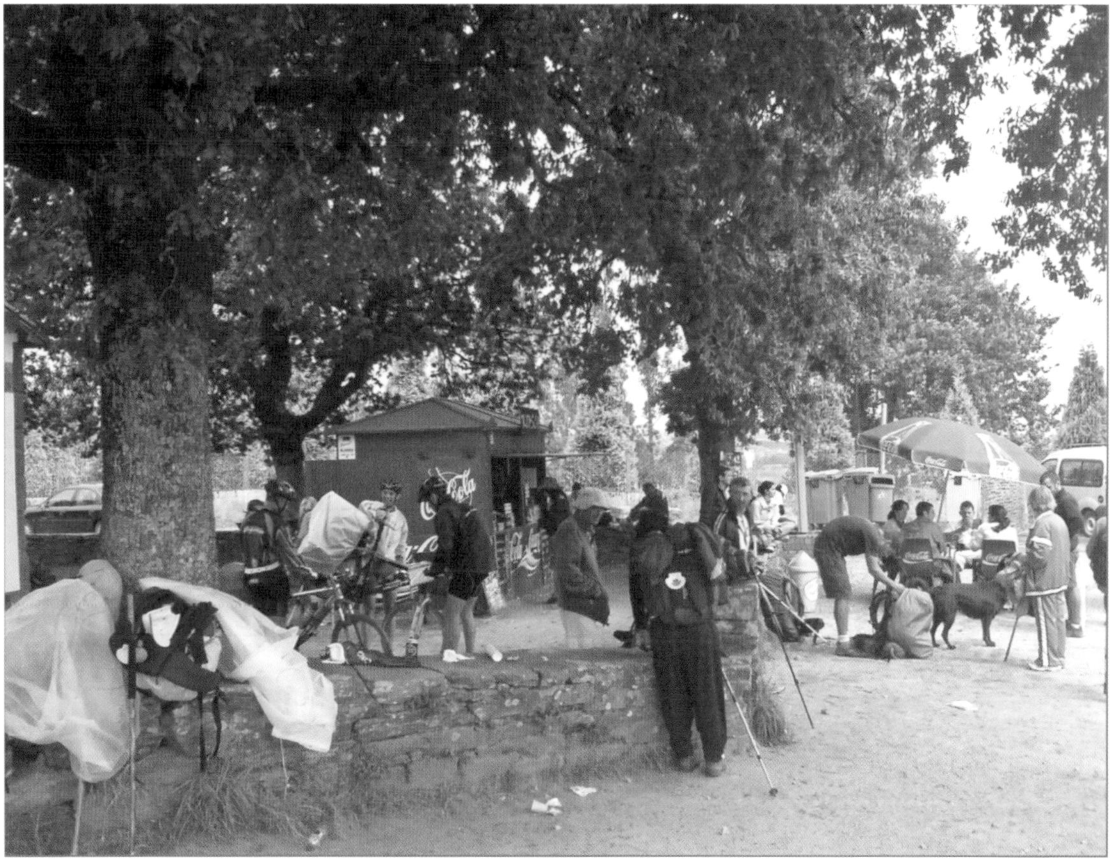

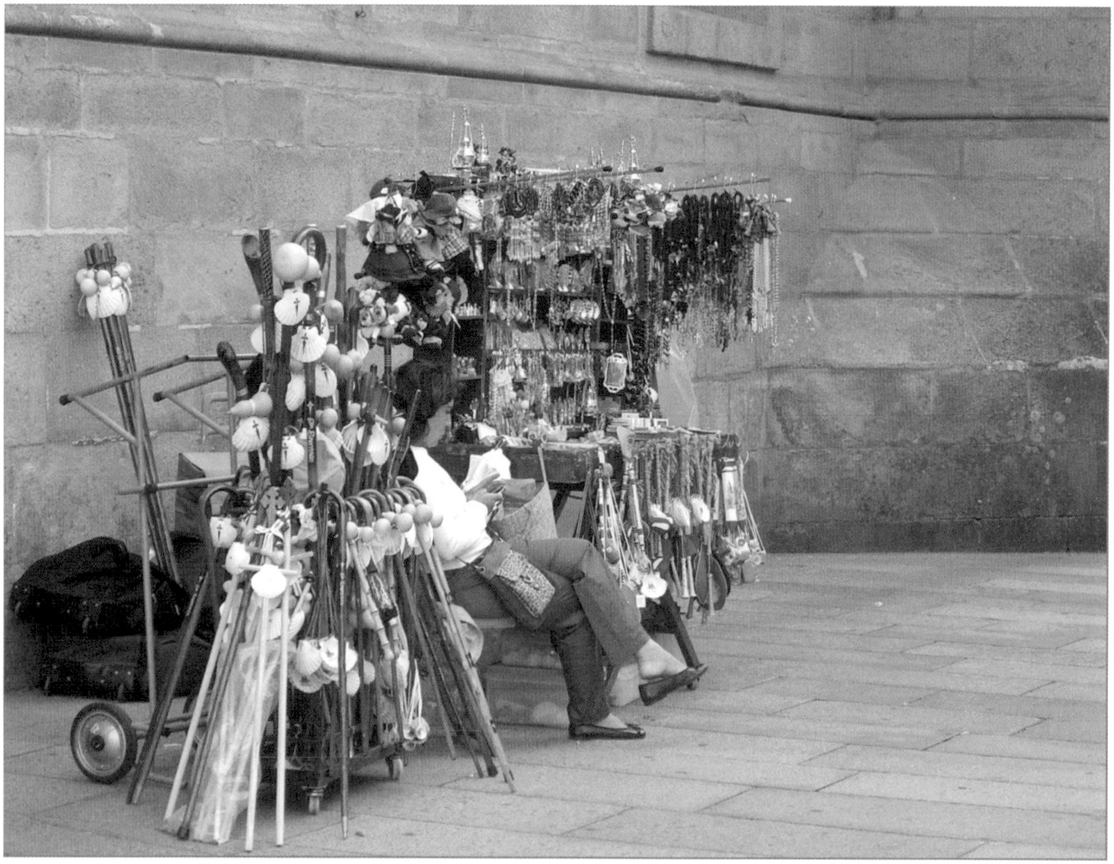

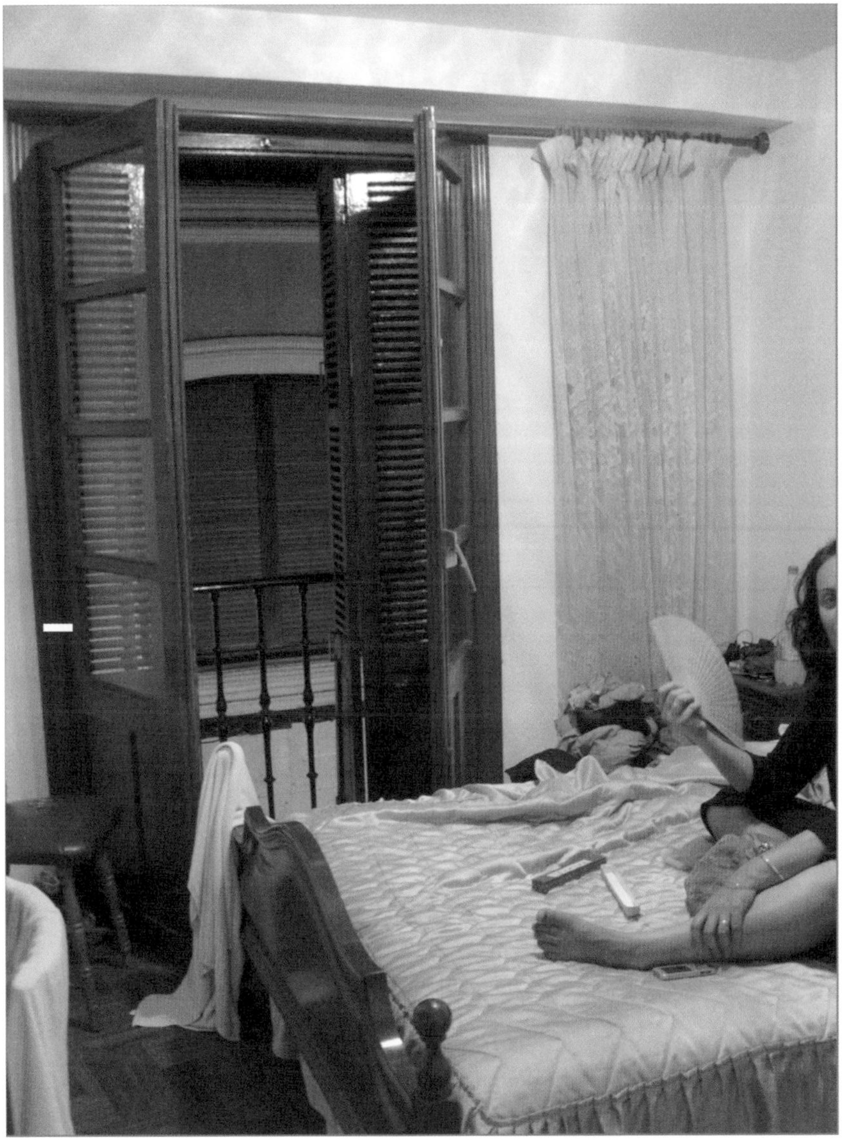

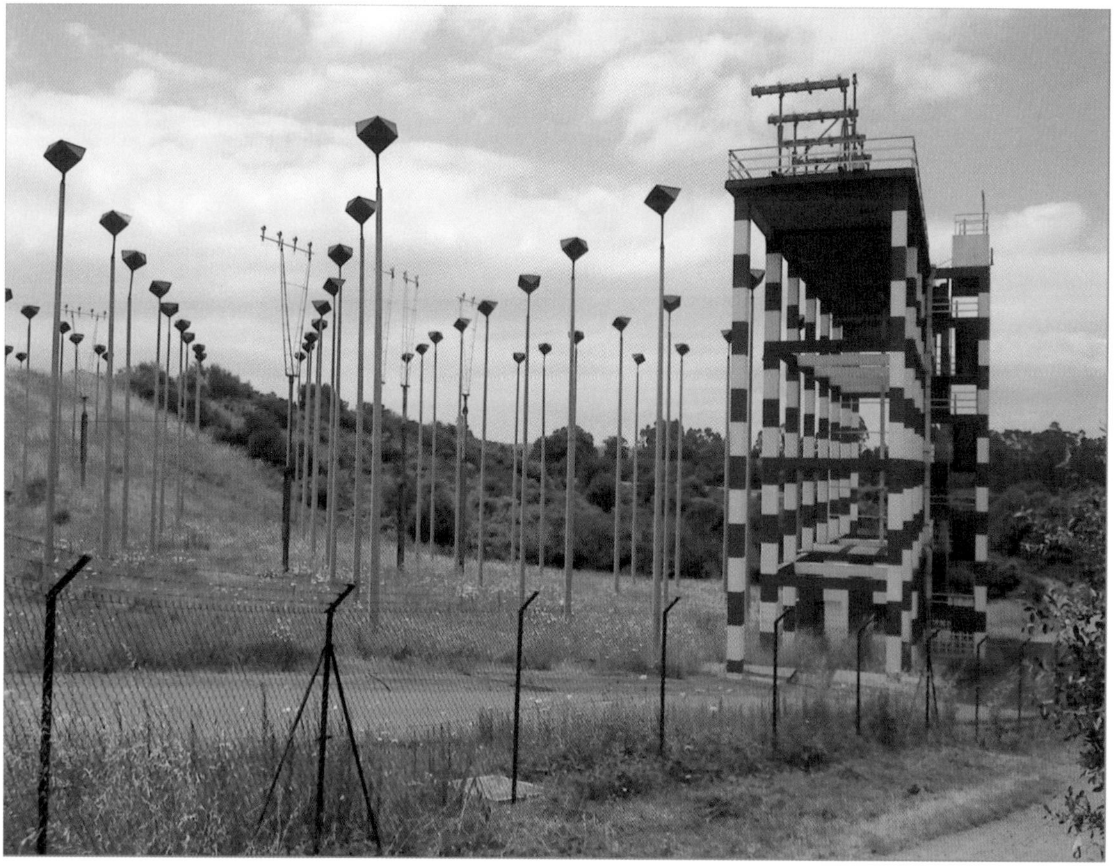

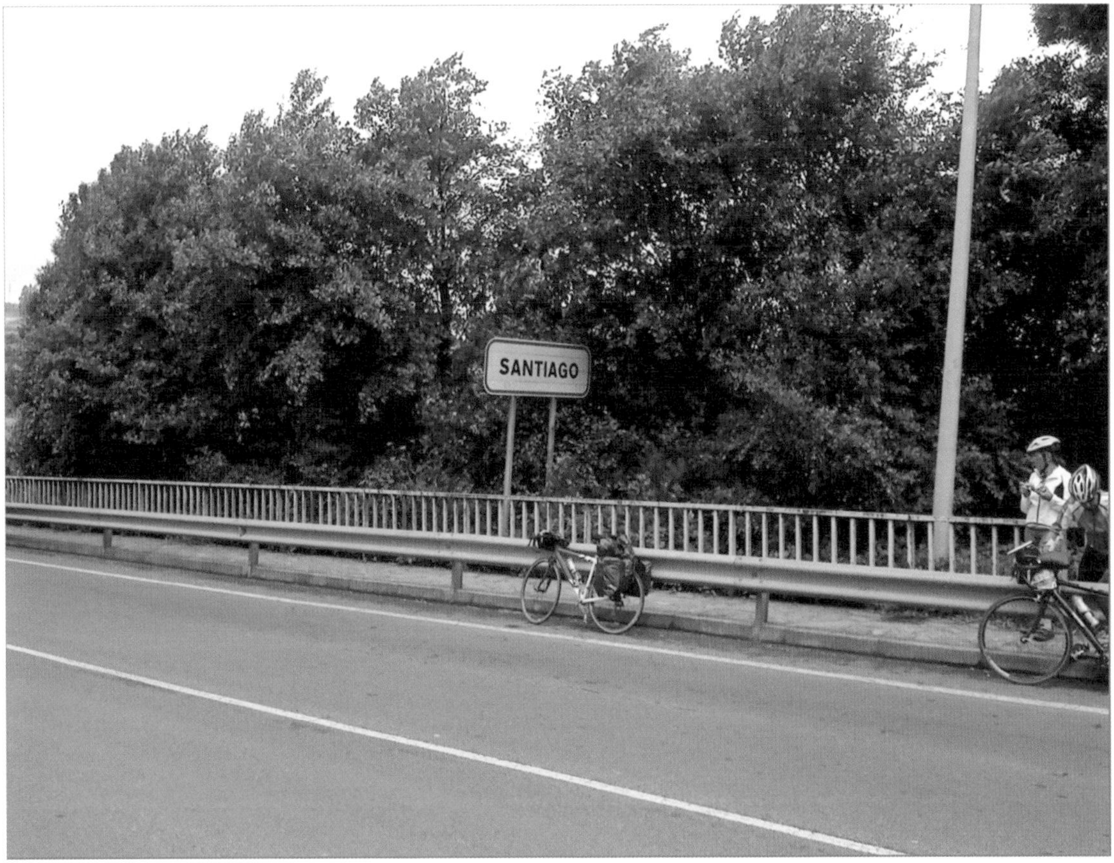
SANTIAGO

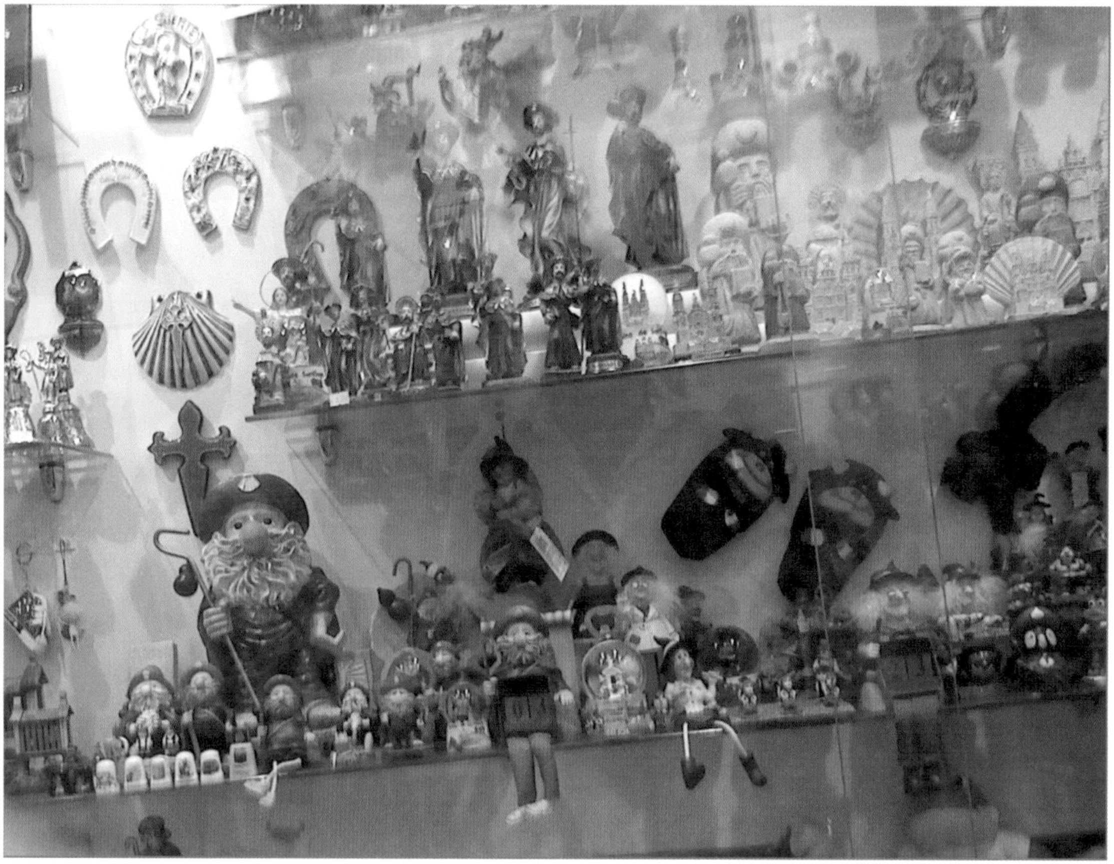

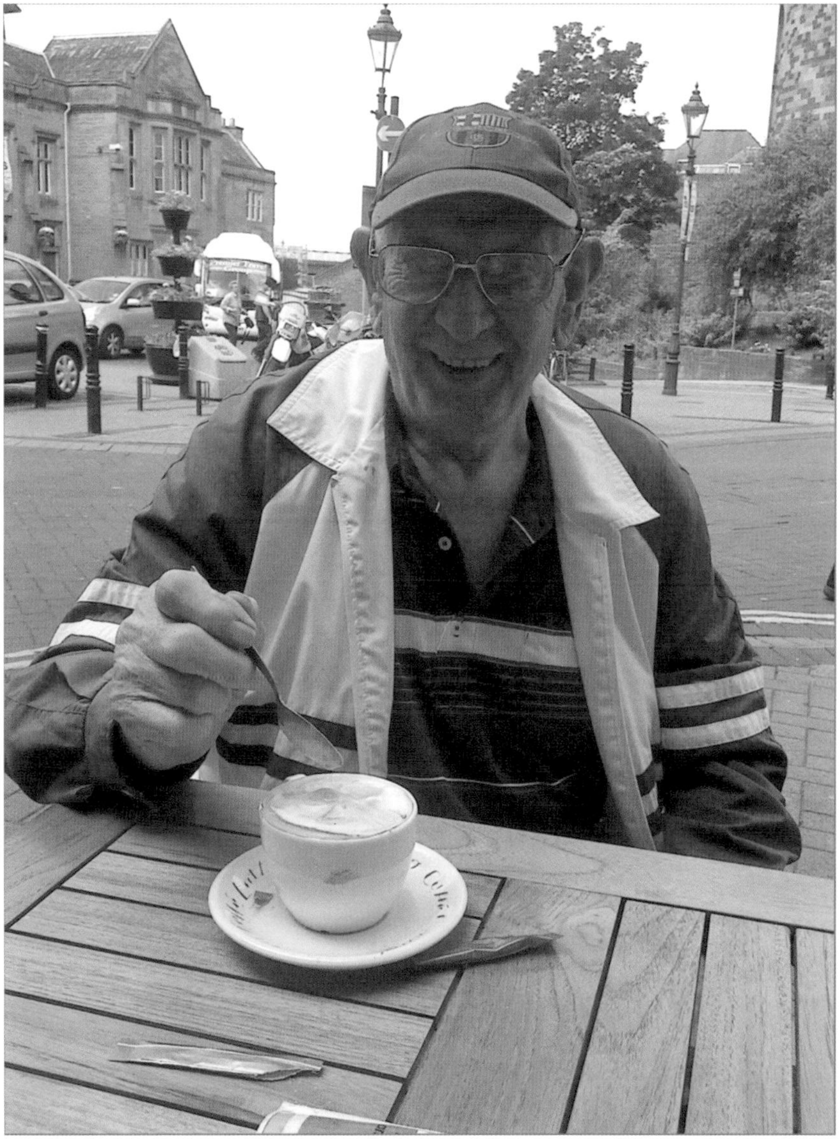

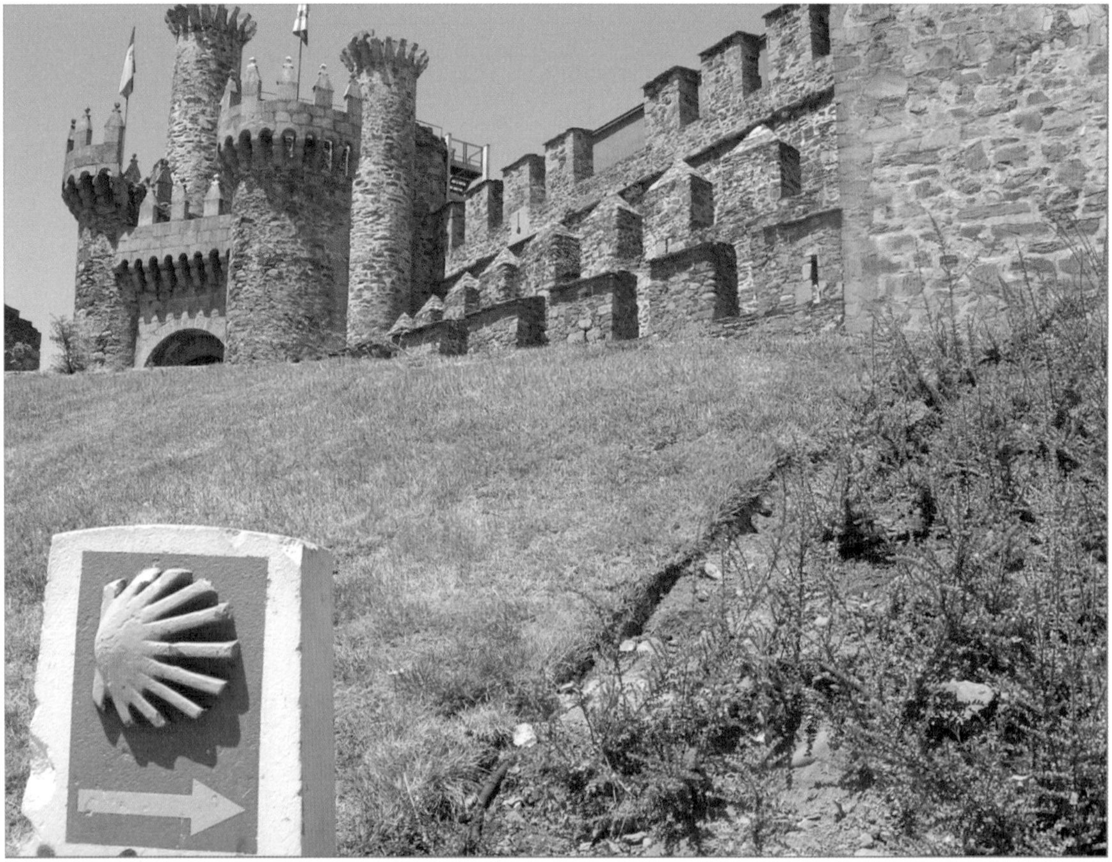

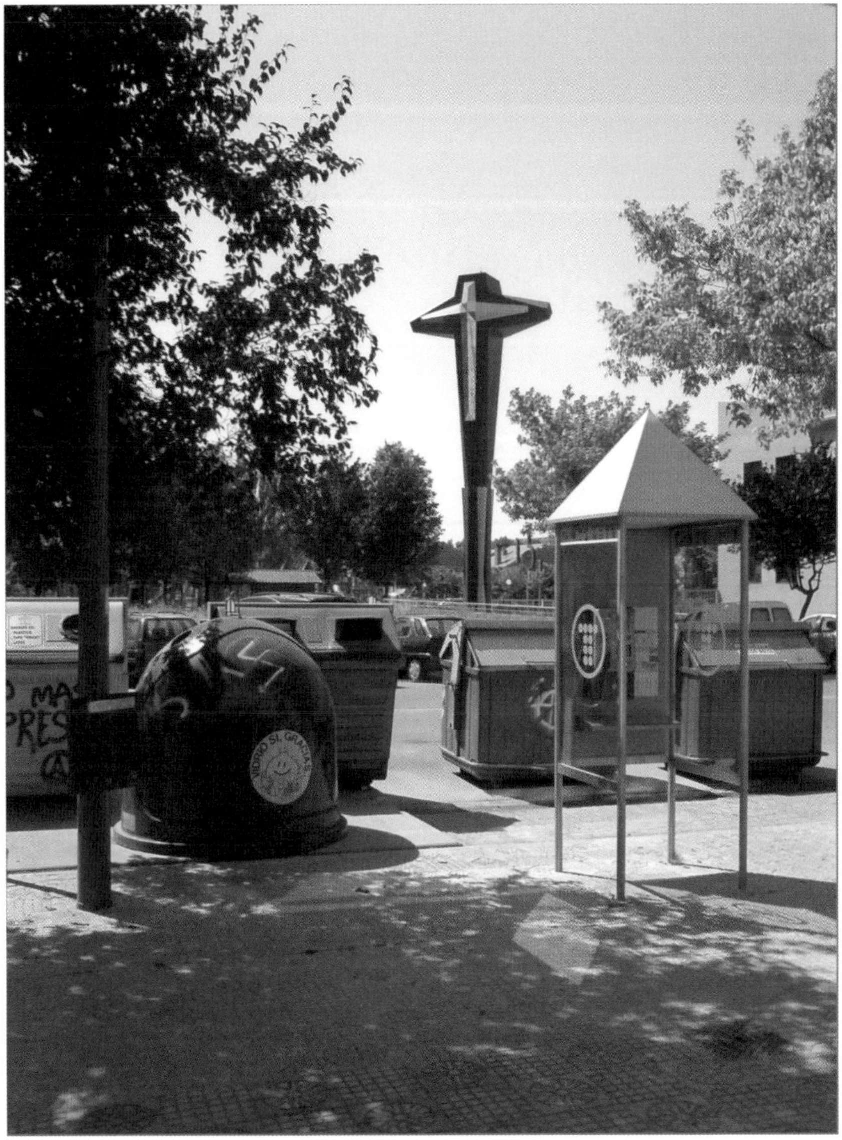
VIDRIO SI, GRACIAS

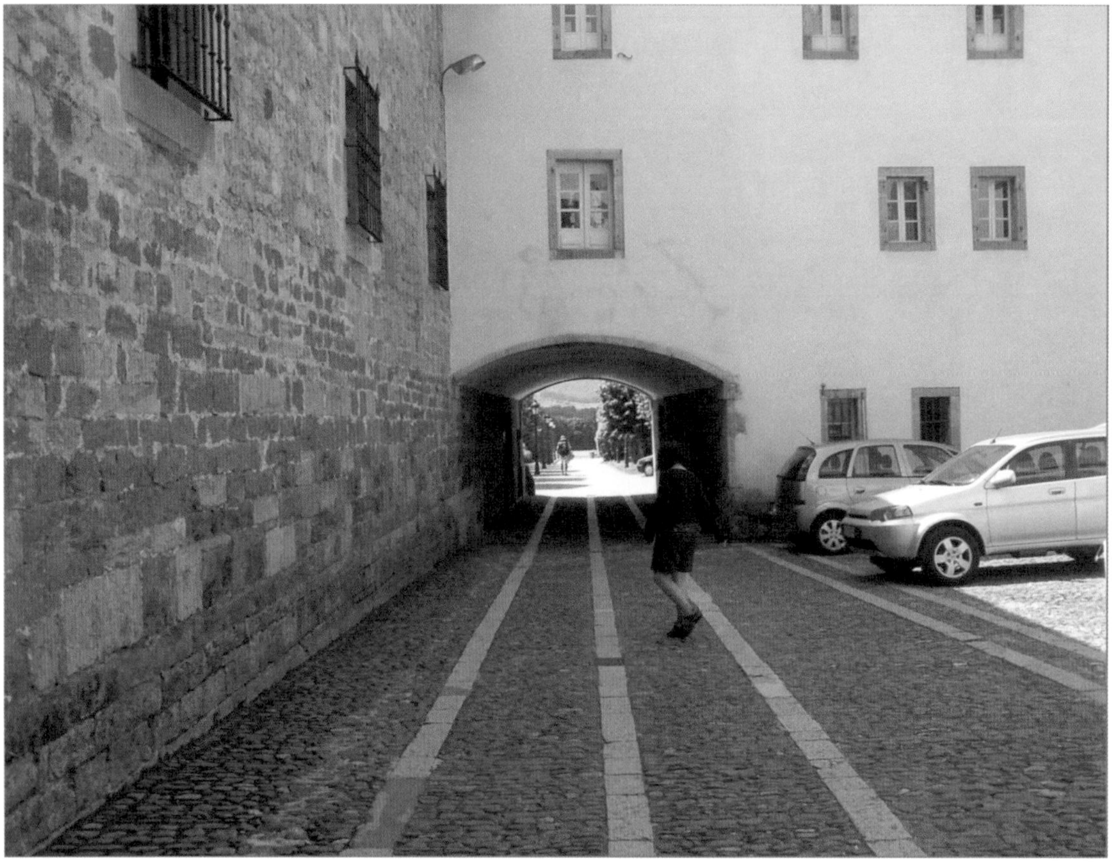

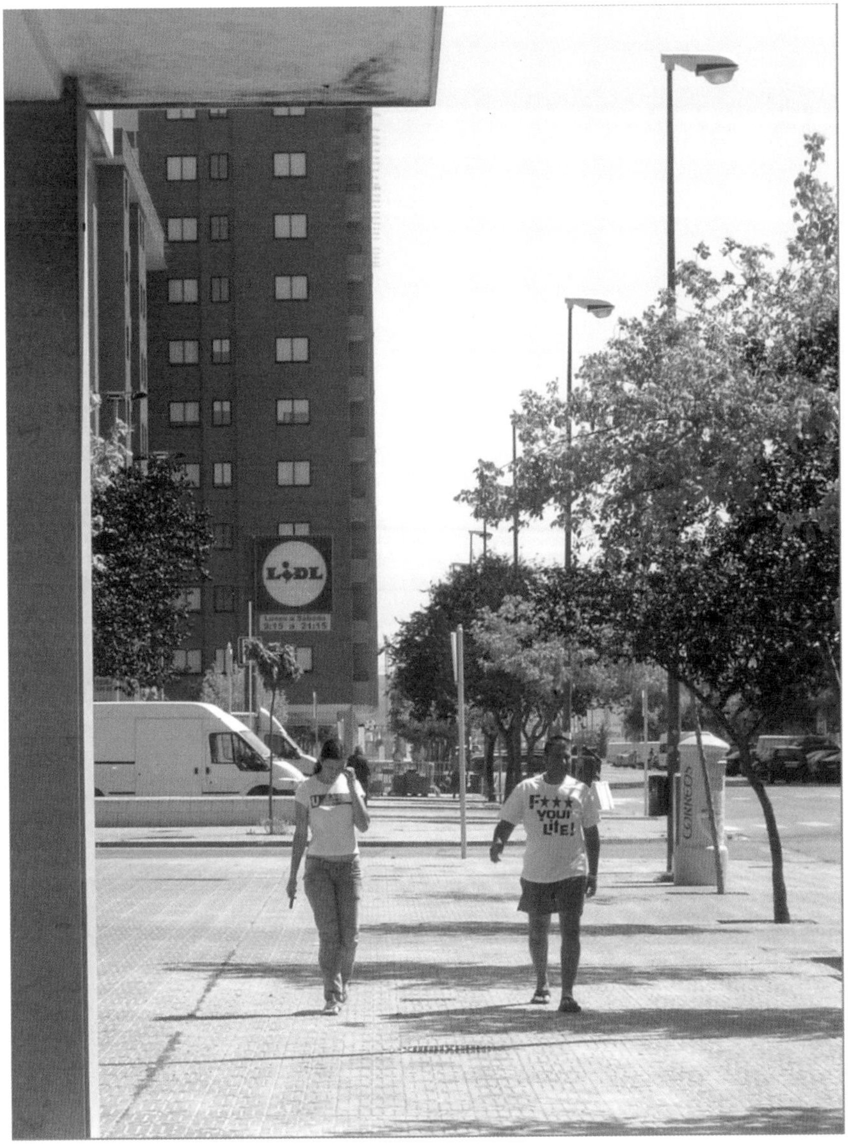
LIDL
F★★★ YOUR LIFE!
CORREOS

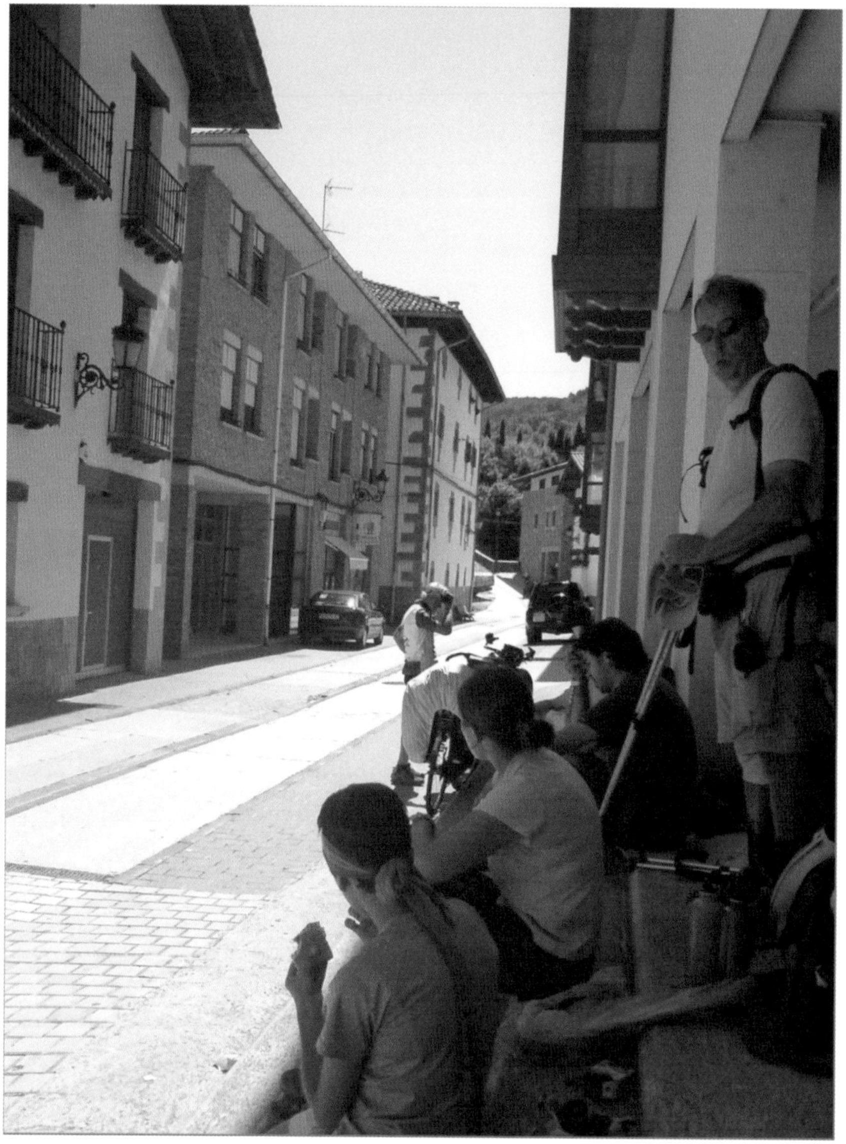

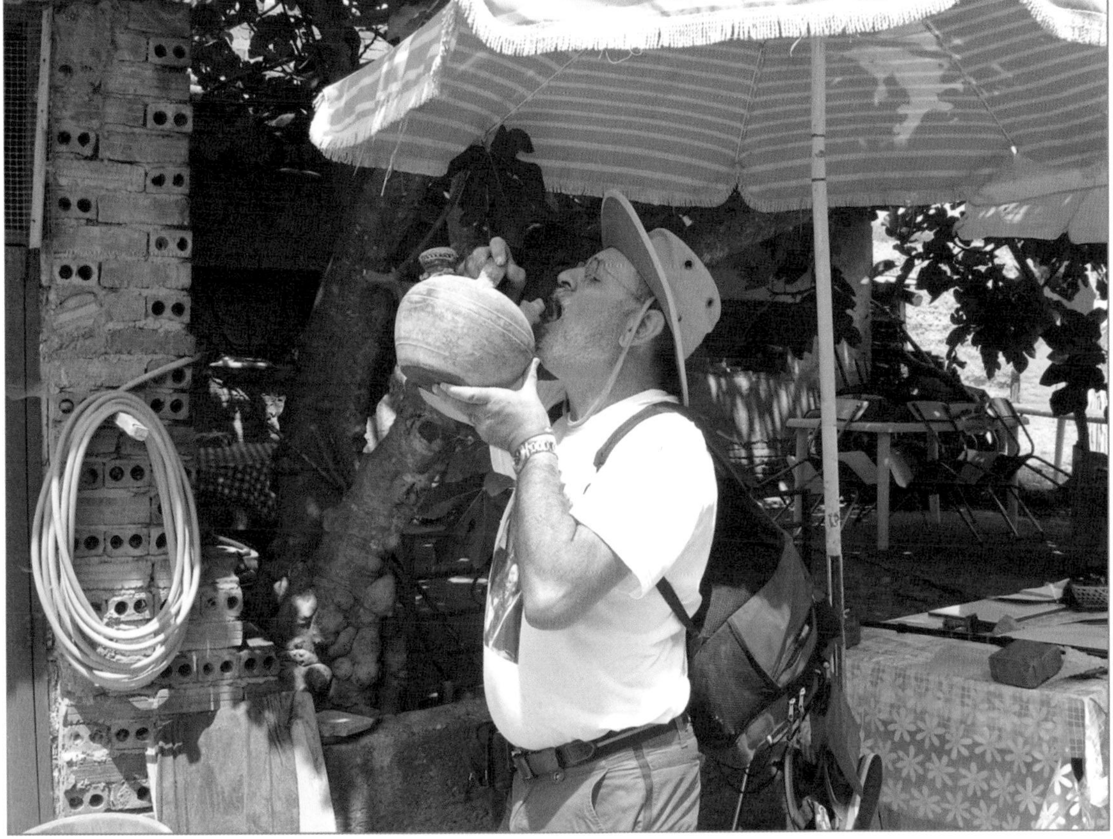

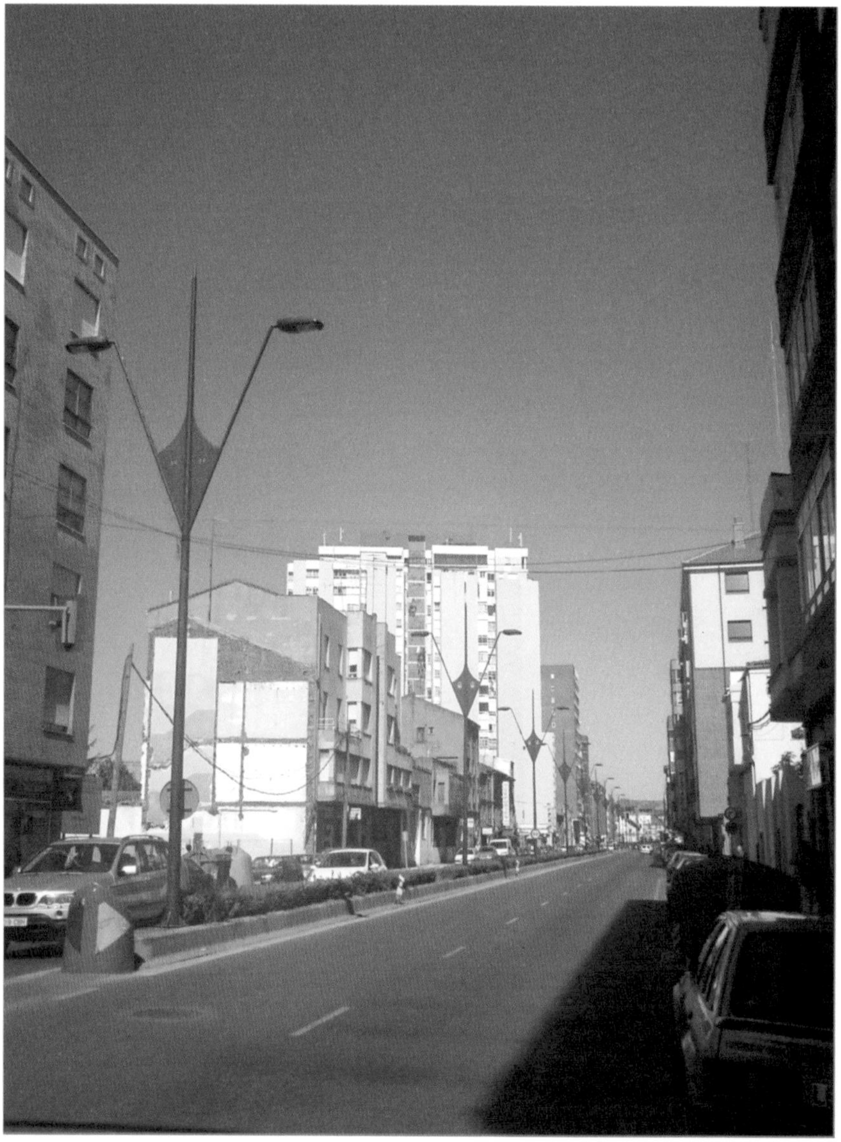

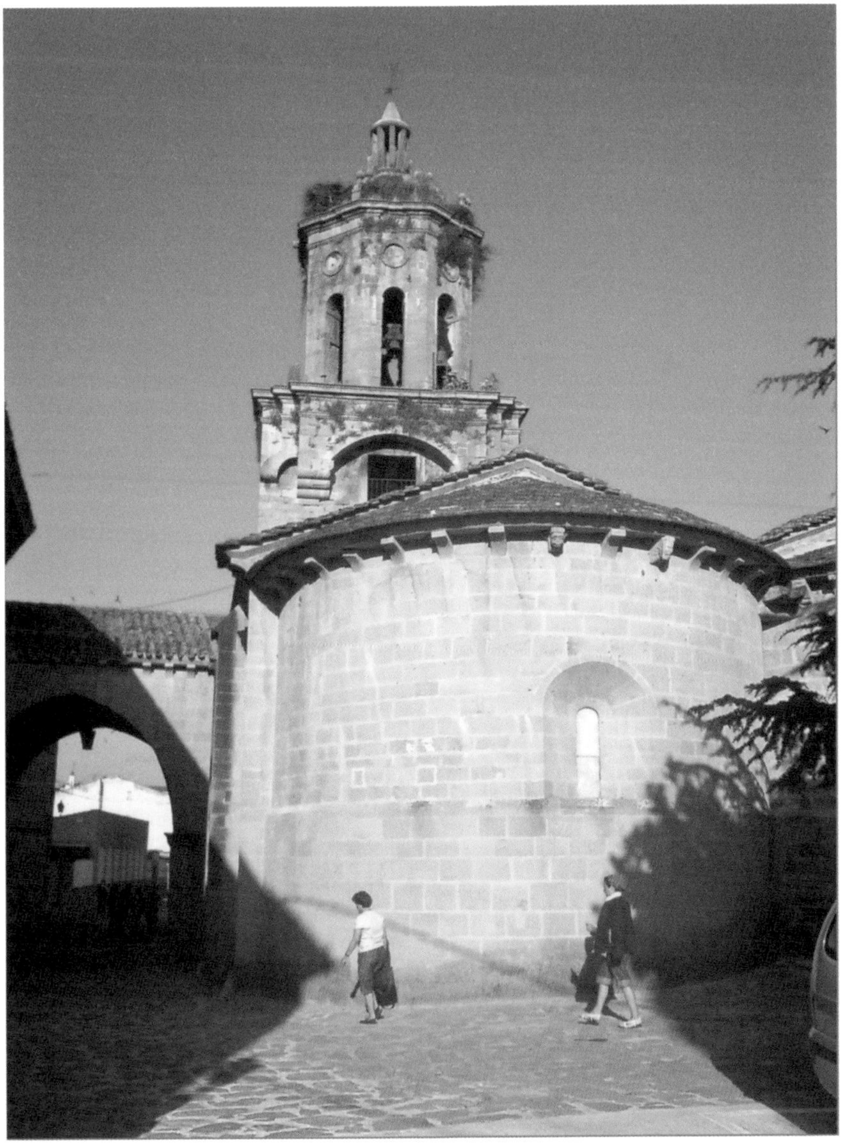

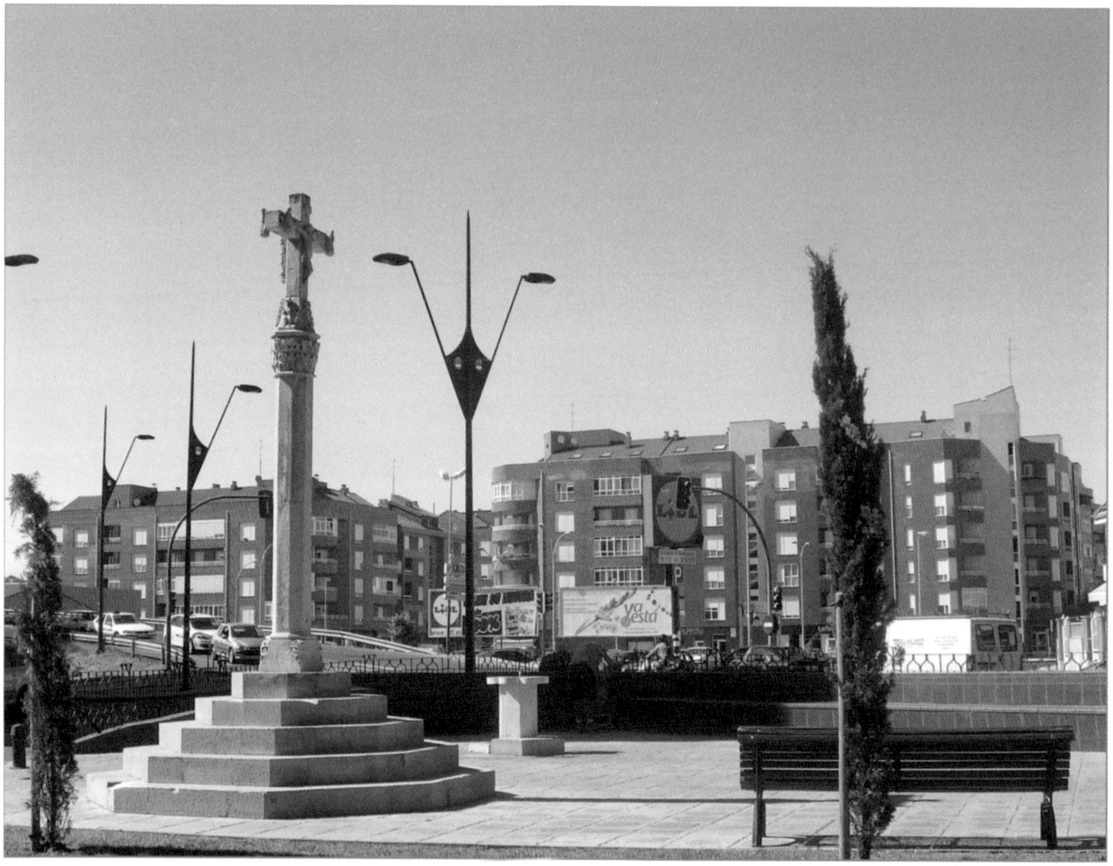

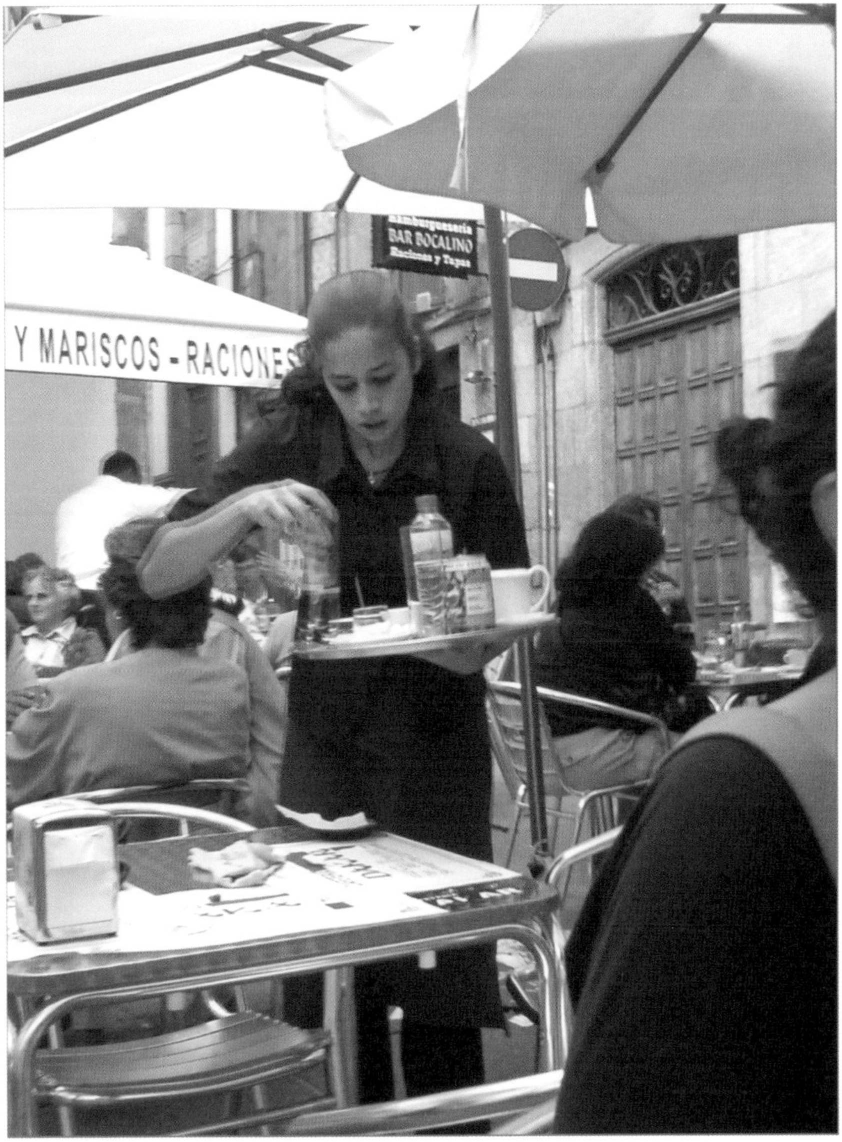
BAR BOCALINO
Raciones y Tapas
Y MARISCOS - RACIONES

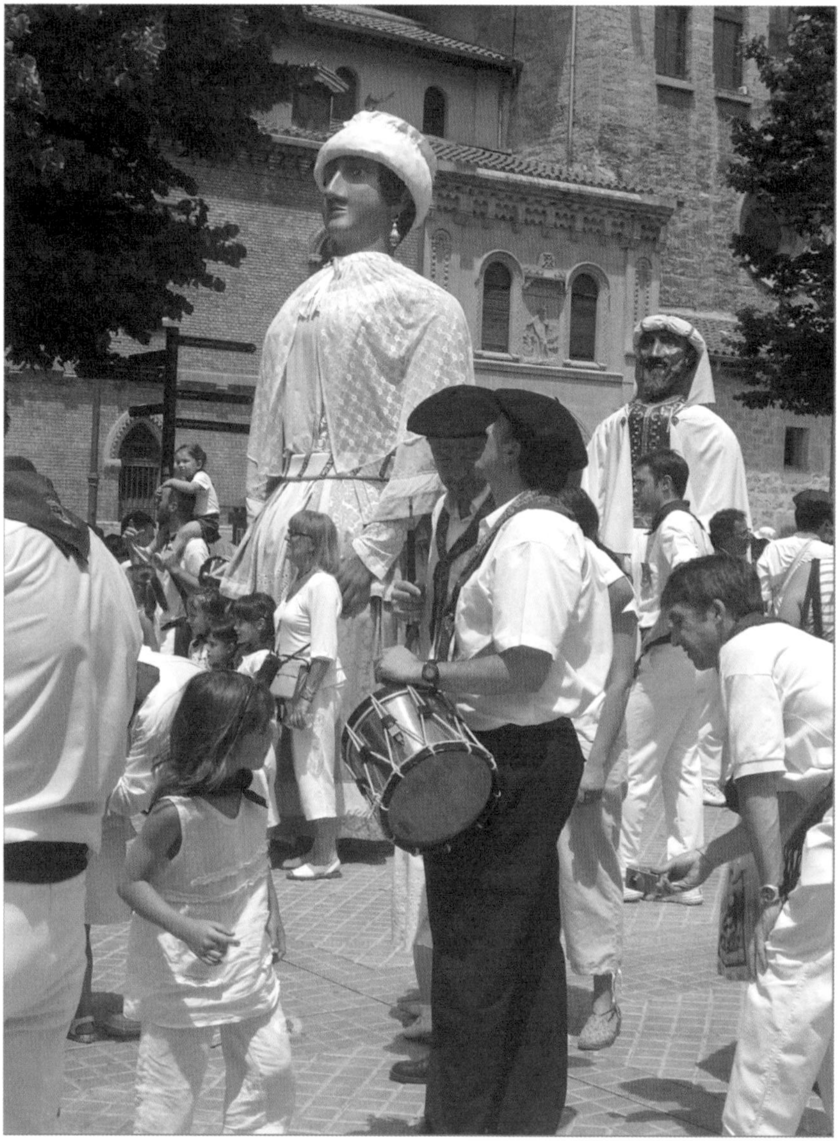

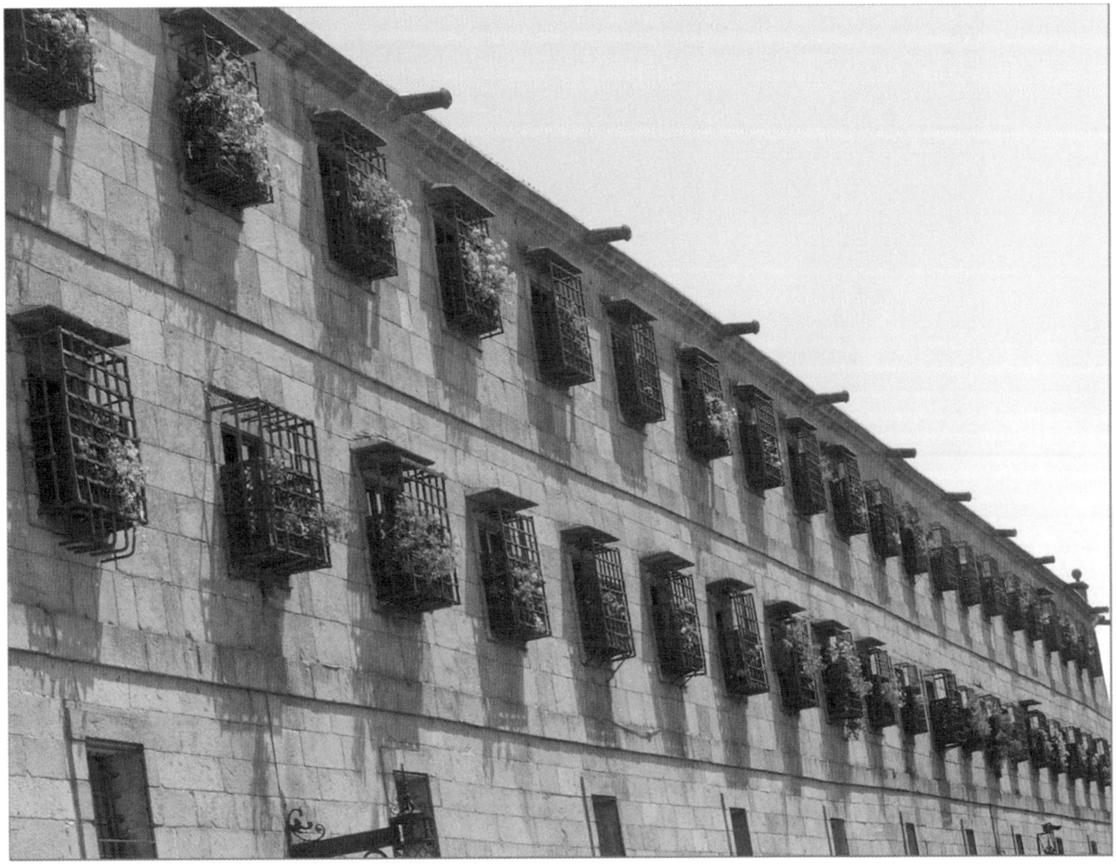

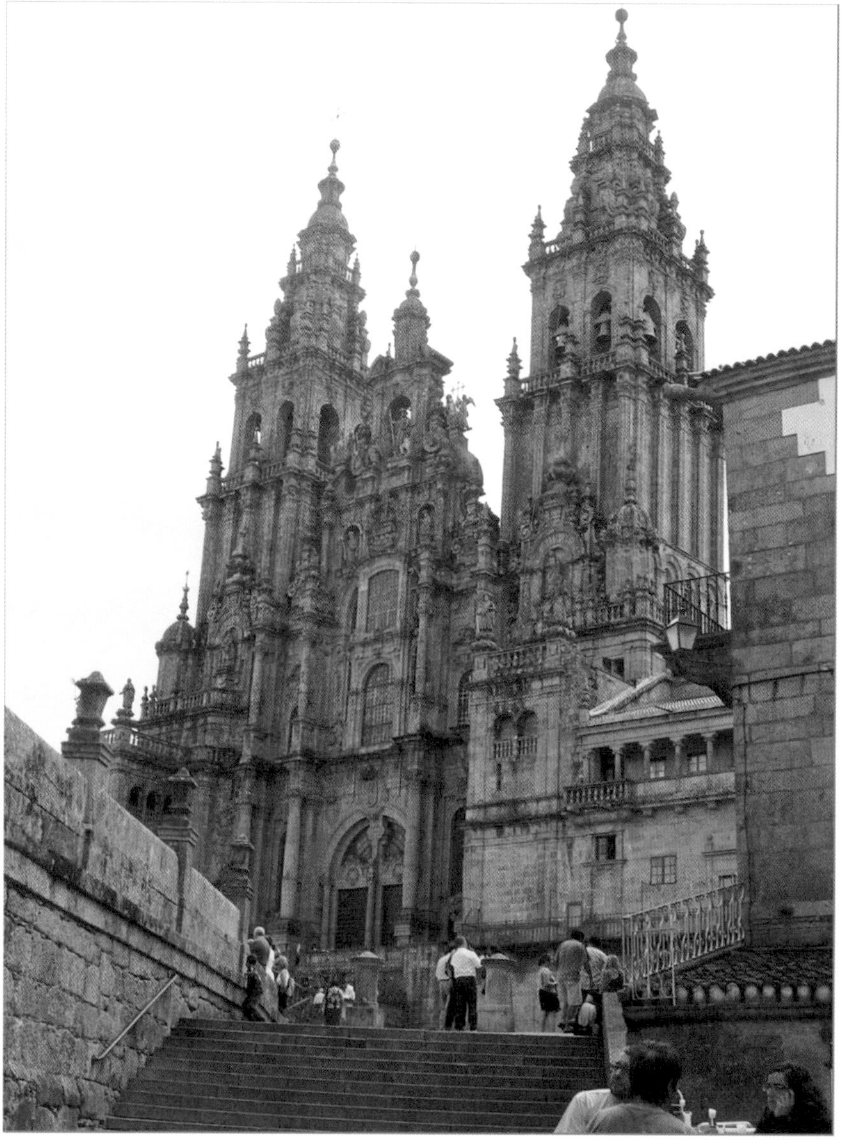

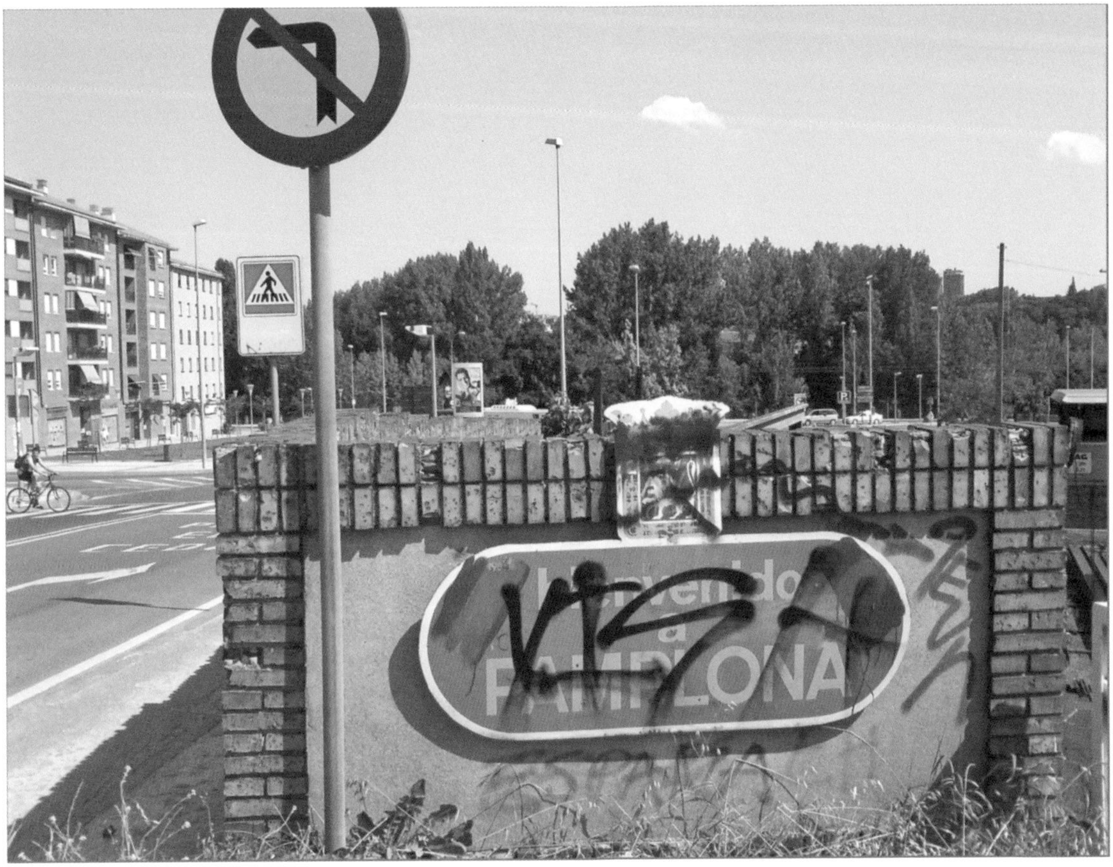
PAMPLONA